Blood and Guts

A Working Guide to Your Own Insides

Written and illustrated by
LINDA ALLISON
Assisted by David Katz, Ph.D.

LITTLE, BROWN AND COMPANY
Boston   Toronto   London

This Brown Paper School book was edited and prepared for publication at The Yolla Bolly Press, Covelo, California, between November 1975 and May 1976. The series is under the supervision of James and Carolyn Robertson.
Production staff members are: Colleen Carter, Sharon Miley, and Gene Floyd.

Library of Congress Cataloging in Publication Data

Allison, Linda.
    Blood and guts.

    (The brown paper school)
    SUMMARY: Discusses the elements of the human body. Includes suggestions for related experiments and projects.
    1. Human physiology — Juvenile literature. 2. Anatomy, Human — Juvenile literature. [1. Physiology. 2. Anatomy, Human] I. Title.
QP37.A52   612   76-17839
ISBN 0-316-03442-8
ISBN 0-316-03443-6 pbk.

Many of the experiments in this book
were tried out by the kids in the Kensington Science Club
on their own insides (and outsides).
Thanks, kids.

You Are Many Things

You are miles of blood vessels, billions of cells, hundreds of muscles, thousands of hairs, quarts of blood.

You are a system of levers, pumps, and bellows.

You are electrical charges and chemical reactions.

You are a furnace, filters, and a fancy computer with a vast memory bank.

You are a finely tuned organism with more living parts than New York City, all operating in harmony.

When you think about it, you are pretty incredible.

This is a guidebook to help you explore the amazing territory within your own skin.

This is not a sit-back-and-listen book. It is a do-it-yourself, get-acquainted guide to your own anatomy. So make sure to stop, look, listen, thump, poke, and test as you work your way through this book.

This book does not cover every subject. It's not meant to be read in any special order. There are lots of starting places where you can dig in and get excited. This book does not have all the answers. When you have questions, you can take them to the library, where there are plenty of hefty body books with more information.

So get started and have fun and be prepared to be amazed at your own insides. You are blood and guts — and a whole lot more.

What's in this Book

SCIENCE TALK

This book uses a lot of science words you've probably never met before. These words may look a little weird, like a foreign language or something. They usually are a foreign language. Mostly Latin and Greek.

In the old days, and even still, scientists have named their discoveries using Greek or Latin. They were considered to be the languages that learned persons in any country would know.

Whether you study guts, guppies, or morning glories, you are likely to run into some proper Latin terms. In this book these words and other hard ones get special treatment. The first time they are used, they are in *italic letters*. Then there is a how-to-say-it guide different from the dictionary's. This is sometimes not quite as precise, but it's a lot easier to understand.

You already know a lot of Latin words, like plus, sub-, in-, ex-, aquarium, coliseum, gymnasium.

So don't let these weird words scare you. If you scratch the surface of an English word, you are likely to find Latin roots anyway.

MAKING ALLOWANCES

Everybody is the same.

Each of us has a pair of eyes, lungs, and thumbs. We have skin and shins. We bleed when we get cut. Everybody eats and excretes.

But, everybody is not the same.

A person can be tall, round, or muscle-bound. Some can wiggle their ears. Some are curly-haired, some are straight-haired. Some are fast walkers. Some are fast talkers.

So when you do the activities in this book, leave room for a lot of differences. It's vast diversity that gives living things the tool kit to survive in an ever-changing world.

Skin

THE BAG YOU LIVE IN

The first creatures on earth were sea creatures. They were protected from the sun's rays by a blanket of ocean. Under water they remained cool and moist. The seas they swam were rich in nutrients and minerals. The skin that separated them from their outside world was rather simple, since their insides were very much like their outsides.

Since the earliest days, our environment and our skins have changed considerably. Inside your body, cells live bathed in a fluid environment much like the ancient seas. Outside your body's skin is air, a gaseous space, full of drying winds and radiation from the sun. A dangerous environment for a creature who is 60% water.

Your skin's main job is to serve as a water-tight container, preventing your internal sea from drying up.

Besides keeping water in, skin keeps things out. Skin provides protection from bacteria, dirt, and the sun's rays.

Skin is an important part of your body's climate control system. Sweating, goose bumps, and simple heat loss from the skin all help keep your internal temperature comfortable.

Skin is also a sensor; thousands of nerve endings in the skin keep you informed of events outside.

Climate Control

Mammals, warm-blooded creatures like ourselves, are very fussy about their internal temperatures, and with good reason. A few degrees can mean the difference between life and death.

A very important job for the bag you live in is to make sure its contents are kept at a comfortable temperature. Skin does this two ways: by radiation and by evaporation.

When your internal temperature rises, your brain signals your blood to step up circulation to the skin. (You have a whole system of tiny blood vessels just underneath the skin's surface.) In this way, the body's internal heat is carried by the blood to the surface, where it is lost by radiation.

Meanwhile, the sweat glands spring into action, and perspiration is released through the pores. This liquid evaporates on your skin and you cool off.

When your temperature drops, your brain signals that heat must now be saved. Less blood circulates to the skin, and sweating stops.

Suppose you had a hot can of coke. If you leave it alone, it will cool down. That's radiation. If you're in a hurry for it to cool, you could cover it with a damp cloth. That's evaporation.

Evaporation   If you have a hard time believing evaporation keeps you cool, try this:

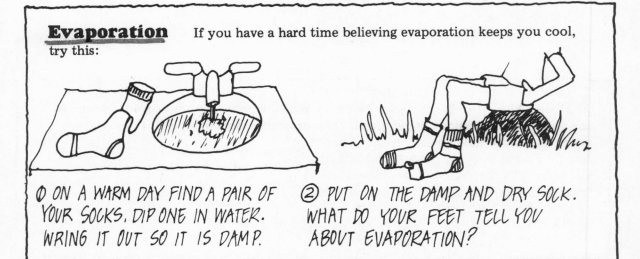

① ON A WARM DAY FIND A PAIR OF YOUR SOCKS. DIP ONE IN WATER. WRING IT OUT SO IT IS DAMP.

② PUT ON THE DAMP AND DRY SOCK. WHAT DO YOUR FEET TELL YOU ABOUT EVAPORATION?

Quick Cool   The rate of evaporation has a direct effect on your temperature. This is something your skin is very sensitive to. Test a friend's skin with two liquids that have different rates of evaporation.

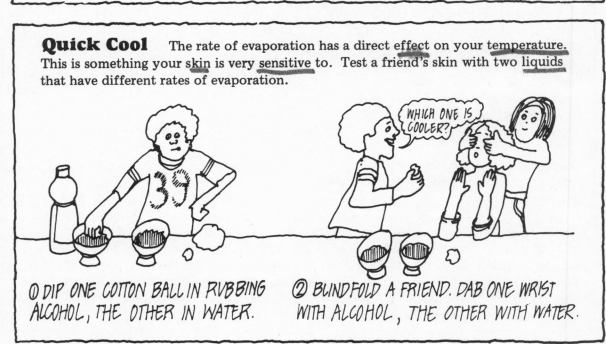

① DIP ONE COTTON BALL IN RUBBING ALCOHOL, THE OTHER IN WATER.

② BLINDFOLD A FRIEND. DAB ONE WRIST WITH ALCOHOL, THE OTHER WITH WATER.

It's Not the Heat — It's the Humidity

On a humid day the air is already full of water and is unwilling to accept more. The perspiration on your skin tends to stay on your skin rather than evaporating into the air.

80% humidity means the air contains 80% of the water it can hold. At this humidity your cooling system has slowed way down and is operating at about 20% efficiency. No wonder you're sticky and warm!

THE BODY CAN STAND DRY HEAT OF UP TO 200°F FOR SEVERAL HOURS WITH NO ILL EFFECTS. AT 100% HUMIDITY, THE BODY TEMERATURE WILL RISE WHEN THE OUTSIDE DEGREES EXCEED 90°F.

Sweaty Palms

About two million of the pores in your skin are connected to sweat-making glands. Sweat glands are more concentrated in certain skin areas. Here is a test to help locate yours.

½ CUP WATER 2 SPOONS CORN STARCH, STIR WELL

① MAKE SOME TEST PAPERS. CUT UP SOME WRITING PAPER. DIP THE SHEETS IN CORN STARCH SOLUTION. LET THEM DRY.

② PAINT YOUR PALM WITH IODINE. (MAKE SURE TO KEEP IT OUT OF THE REACH OF YOUR YOUNGER BROTHERS OR SISTERS.)

③ DO SOMETHING TO WORK UP A SWEAT.

④ PRESS THE PAPER TO YOUR PAINTED PALM. SWEAT GLANDS WILL SHOW UP AS DARK SPOTS.

Skin Prints   If you think your skin is simple, look again. Your skin does a number of jobs and has a number of appearances. It is both thick and thin, light and dark, smooth and wrinkled. Skin prints are a way to take a closer look at the bag you live in.

① RUB SOME SOFT PENCIL LEAD ONTO A SHEET OF PAPER, UNTIL YOU GET A BIG BLACK BLOB.

② PICK UP A GOOD SMUDGE ON YOUR FINGER.

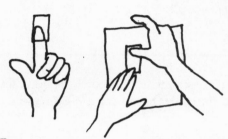

③ CAREFULLY PICK UP THE SMUDGE WITH A PIECE OF SCOTCH TAPE. PULL IT AWAY AND PRESS IT ONTO A CLEAN PAPER.

④ SEE HOW MANY KINDS OF SKIN PRINTS YOU CAN FIND ON YOUR OWN BODY.

Skin Deep

Skin is made up of layers, rather like a birthday cake.

The under layer is called the *dermis* (DUR miss). It is alive and contains blood vessels, glands, nerve cells, and hair roots. (Under the dermis is a layer of fat and connecting tissue.)

The layer on top is the *epidermis* (epp-e DUR miss), the skin's outer limits. This is made up of layers of dead cells.

Skin cells in the dermis are constantly growing and being pushed to the surface.

There they die and form the dead outer layer. The dead outer cells are rubbed off in little bits. In this way your skin reconstructs itself every few weeks.

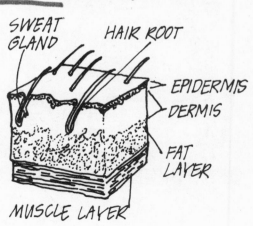

SWEAT GLAND

HAIR ROOT

EPIDERMIS

DERMIS

FAT LAYER

MUSCLE LAYER

Cleavage Lines

If your skin is punctured with a round instrument like a nail, it leaves a hole. However, it doesn't leave a round hole. It leaves a slit. Surgeons have made maps of these slit patterns, or cleavage lines. They generally follow the crease marks on the skin, and are about the same for most bodies. Skin that is cut along a cleavage line rather than across has a much less likely chance of leaving a scar.

Birthday Suit

Your skin is a suit with many surfaces. It is damp, dry, thick, thin, hairy, and smooth. It is pleated to give you room to move. It's the last word in all-purpose suits.

SMOOTH AND WET LININGS

TOUGH, CLEAR CORNEA.

PLEATS AND FOLDS OVER KNUCKLES AND JOINTS

TOUGH KERATIN NAILS, CUTTERS AND SHIELDERS

TRACKS AND RIDGES FOR GRIPPING

SPOTS THICKEN WHERE WEAR IS THE HEAVIEST. SKIN MAY BE A THICK 3/16" ON THE SOLES, OR A THIN 1/500" OVER THE EYES.

Keeping in Touch

Your skin lies between you and the outside world. It is in a position to tell you a lot about what is going on out there. It does so with a vast network of nerve endings that sit just under your tough outside hide.

Remember, skin comes in two basic sections: the living, growing dermis and the dead epidermis.

Your surface skin is a kind of protective glove, but it's thin enough to allow your nerve endings to be excited by outside events.

Touch is no simple sense. You are able to feel warm, squishy, thick, furry, fat, mushy, hard, slimy, freezing cold, greasy, hot, dry, cracked, and on and on.

This whole sensational range is felt by four basic kinds of sensors. Your skin is equipped with sensors for heat, cold, pressure, and pain.

Sensations are often combinations of two or more kinds of information.

Getting kissed is a combination of pressure and heat. Getting kicked is a combination of pressure and pain.

Map the Back of Your Hand

Not every part of your skin is equipped with all four sensors. Some parts of your skin can feel the prick of a pin while others can't. Impossible? Feeling is believing.

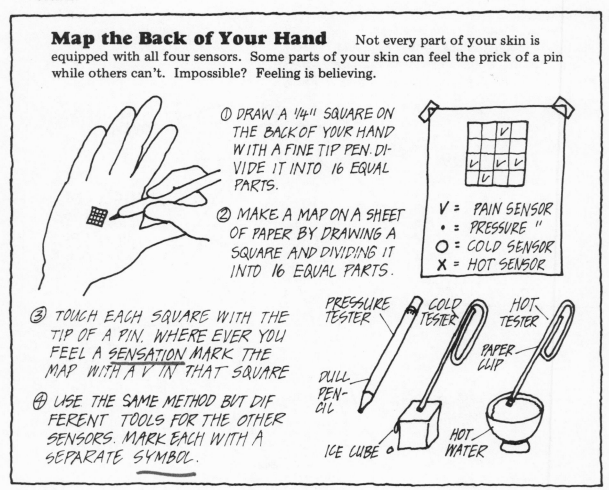

① DRAW A ¼" SQUARE ON THE BACK OF YOUR HAND WITH A FINE TIP PEN. DIVIDE IT INTO 16 EQUAL PARTS.

② MAKE A MAP ON A SHEET OF PAPER BY DRAWING A SQUARE AND DIVIDING IT INTO 16 EQUAL PARTS.

V = PAIN SENSOR
• = PRESSURE "
O = COLD SENSOR
X = HOT SENSOR

③ TOUCH EACH SQUARE WITH THE TIP OF A PIN. WHERE EVER YOU FEEL A SENSATION MARK THE MAP WITH A V IN THAT SQUARE

④ USE THE SAME METHOD BUT DIFFERENT TOOLS FOR THE OTHER SENSORS. MARK EACH WITH A SEPARATE SYMBOL.

PRESSURE TESTER
COLD TESTER
HOT TESTER
PAPER CLIP
DULL PENCIL
ICE CUBE
HOT WATER

. . . Like the Back of Your Hand

Most people think they know the back of their hands fairly well. But did you know that a ¾-inch-square patch of skin, which is only about one-twentieth of an inch thick, contains:

9 feet of blood vessels
600 pain sensors

30 hairs
300 sweat glands
4 oil glands
13 yards of nerves
9000 nerve endings
6 cold sensors
36 heat sensors
75 pressure sensors

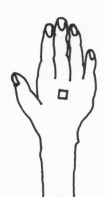

Touchy Points

Your skin is not uniformly sensitive. Some spots have many nerve endings, while other places have few. You might have a few ideas about the sensitive spots. Here is how to prove your theory. Try it with a friend. The results may be surprising.

① MAKE A DEVICE TO TEST POINT DISCRIMINATION; CUT A PIECE OF CARDBOARD. MARK IT OFF AS SHOWN.

2½"

⅛" ½" 1" 2"

¼" ¾" 1½"

1"

STICK IN THE PINS.

NOW, DO YOU FEEL ONE POINT?

② WITH THE PINS AT 2", GENTLY PRESS THE DEVICE AGAINST THE SKIN. REDUCE THE DISTANCE UNTIL ONLY ONE POINT IS FELT.

SITE	DISTANCE BETWEEN SENSORS
ARM	
LIPS	
KNEE	
PALMS	

③ MAKE A CHART AND KEEP TRACK OF THE RESULTS. WHERE ARE YOUR MOST SENSITIVE SPOTS? IF YOU WERE DESIGNING AN ANIMAL WHERE WOULD YOU PUT THE SENSITIVE PLACES?

Special Events

Goose bumps are one way your body attempts to keep you warm. Your body knows that nothing keeps things warmer than a blanket of air. (The people who make Thermos jars also know this.) One of the body's responses to cold is to cause body hairs to stand on end, to trap an insulating layer of air. This method works well for animals with luxurious covers like bears or birds. However, for humans, who have only a rather spare cover left, the result is mostly bumps.

Shivering is a way to get warm. When muscles contract they give off heat as a by-product of their effort. (A quicker way to warm up would be a run around the block.) When you're cold and can't run, your body switches on the shiver switch. Your muscles spring into action, contracting and relaxing all over your body. Before you know it you're warm.

Hair

Compare mammals and you will find that humans make a poor showing in the hair department. Thin as it is, our hair still performs some important jobs.

Hair is an insulator. The great mass of human hair is found on top of our heads. This is just as it should be. Heads are exposed. The brain material is very sensitive and needs protection from the hot sun. In tropical places where the sun shines fiercely, humans have evolved a woolly sort of hair. Just the thing for forming an insulating cover against the sun's rays.

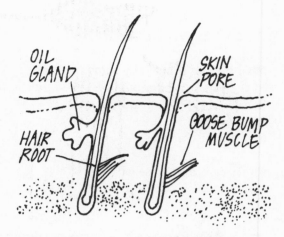

Hair is a protector. It stands guard around body openings to keep all sorts of debris out of our eyes, ears, nose, and mouth (for males anyway).

Hair is a scent trap. It collects smells, especially under arms and around crotches. (A difficult idea to live with in this era, when people spend money trying to smell like flowers.) Scientists think these scents may once have played a larger part in our lives. Some think they might still be important signals. Who knows?

Hair is a sensor. Every hair on your body connects to a nerve. This extends your sense of touch a little beyond your skin — a handy early warning device. Very useful for detecting marauding insects, for example.

18

IN A SQUATTING
POSITION ALL OF
A HUMAN'S HAIRS
POINT DOWNWARDS.
REMEMBER THAT WHEN YOU'RE
CAUGHT IN THE RAIN.

Developing Hairlessness

It is interesting to look at hair patterns in the mammal line of animals. Humans have more skin exposed to the elements than any other land mammal. Tanning, no doubt, is one way our skin compensates for its lack of cover.

Color

Flesh is very sensitive to certain rays in sunlight called ultraviolet rays. Those are the evil burning rays that the suntan oil makers constantly warn you about. Skin has a protective device to keep your cells from being cooked by ultraviolet light. It is called tanning.

When skin is exposed to sunlight, it builds up a shield of protective coloring called *melanin* (MEL a nin). This is what you see as a suntan. It is good to remember that sunbathing is a radiation bath. Unless your skin has built up some melanin, use caution on your first days out in the sun. To forget is certain death for thousands of skin cells.

Flesh?

Skin comes in a variety of colors, and for good reason. Peoples living near the equator are exposed to stronger and more constant sunlight, so their skins have adapted by retaining a lot of protective coloring. The native folk of tropical America, Australia, and Africa all have the rich dark skins of the sun countries.

Pale skins are native to the folk inhabiting regions of weaker sun. Northern skins normally have very little protective coloring. In lands where the sun is scarce, it is better if skin stays transparent so it can drink in the benefits of sunlight (such as the formation of vitamin D).

In English, the color flesh is defined as a light pinkish hue — the color of a Caucasian arm. You might remember that in Africa flesh is an arm of another color.

Hairy Facts

Your hair grows altogether 1000 inches per day. Incredible but true; the average head has 100,000 hairs. Each hair grows 1/100 inch daily. With a little simple arithmetic . . .

— Every hair has a lifespan of 2 to 4 years.

— An eyelash lives about 150 days.

— A head of hair is like a forest. New hairs grow next to old growth. So when all the oldies in an area die, you don't have a bald spot.

— Hairs are arranged in a pattern. They grow in clusters, like scales overlapping on a fish. If you sat in a squatting position, with your hands over your head, all your body hairs would point down.

— Scary enough to make your hair curl? Possibly, if you have curly hair. One of the body's reactions to fright is sweating. Curly hair responds to dampness by getting even curlier.

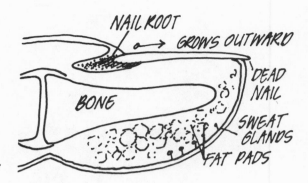

Nails

Nails, like hair, are a specialized part of your skin.

Nails are the human version of claws. While they lack the magnificence of the hooks of an eagle or bear, they are handy when it comes to jobs like picking up dimes.

Nails also do a fine job of serving as hard-hats for your sensitive fingers, as well as for your exposed toes.

Nails are made up of long, tough layers of *keratin* (CARE ah tin). The same protein in a different form makes up your hair.

Bones and Body Plan

THE SHAPE YOU'RE IN

Not all animals have bones.

Worms live perfectly adequate worm lives without a bone in their bodies.

Creatures like crabs have shells. They wear all their bones on the outside.

Humans, however, have their bones on the inside. You can think of your skeleton as a person without any body on it.

Bone Dry?

Your bones are alive. Like other parts of your body, they take in food through the blood, grow, and are repaired. They carry on all the life functions. Only they do so more slowly than most tissues in your body.

30% of bone is living tissue, cells, blood vessels.

45% is mineral deposits, mostly calcium phosphate. This material forms layers of crystals on the surface of a bone, giving it hardness.

25% is water.

Bone Hard

Bone is amazingly strong for its weight. Bones can stand stresses of up to twenty-four thousand pounds per square inch. A medium-size person out for a stroll puts about twelve thousand pounds per square inch on their thighbone with every step.

Reflect for a moment on a thighbone. It is long and thin. Just the thing for a long efficient stride, but not too heavy to lift because it's hollow inside.

Its cylinderlike shape is no accident. The cylinder is one of nature's strongest forms. Coated with layers of rock hard mineral, this long, thin shape is strong indeed.

The ends of the thighbone flare out and are spongy on the inside. This enables them to act as shock absorbers.

A clever design job, but you should expect perfection. ~~After all, nature has had millions of years to practice.~~ In fact, your own bony frame can undergo changes, depending upon how you use it. For example, athletes tend to put a lot of stress on their bones and muscles. Their bones respond to this extra stress by growing larger in certain bone locations where the stress is particularly high.

God is a Master Designer

FEMUR OF AN OFFICE WORKER

FEMUR OF AN ATHLETE

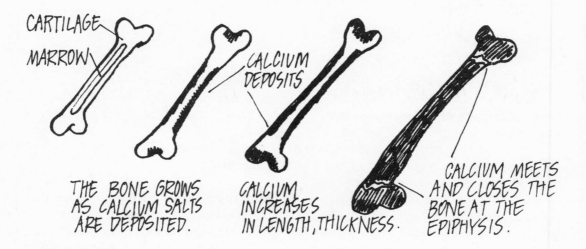

CARTILAGE

MARROW

CALCIUM DEPOSITS

THE BONE GROWS AS CALCIUM SALTS ARE DEPOSITED.

CALCIUM INCREASES IN LENGTH, THICKNESS.

CALCIUM MEETS AND CLOSES THE BONE AT THE EPIPHYSIS.

Bone Formation

When you are born, your bones are soft. They are made of a rubbery substance called *cartilage* (KART i laj). The tip of your nose is cartilage. Wiggle it around and you can get an idea of what your bones feel like before they harden.

Soon after birth bones begin to harden. Your body begins to coat the bones with layers of mineral material. This coating is put on in a special way. Calcium phosphate, which is gotten mostly from milk, is the coating material. It is deposited on the bone from the center and builds outward. This process is

called *calcification* (CAL sah fi KAY-shun).

As you get older, some of the inner deposits are dissolved, but then reappear on the outside. This happens in the long hollow bones. The hollow shape provides lightness and a home for bone marrow, which produces blood cells.

Gradually the calcium layer seals. When it closes, bone growth is no longer possible. The last bone to close is the collar bone, between the ages of eighteen and twenty-five.

Knot a Bone

You can tie a bone in a knot. How? By removing the mineral salts and reducing the bone to its underlying cartilage material. To do it you will need some acid and some adult help.

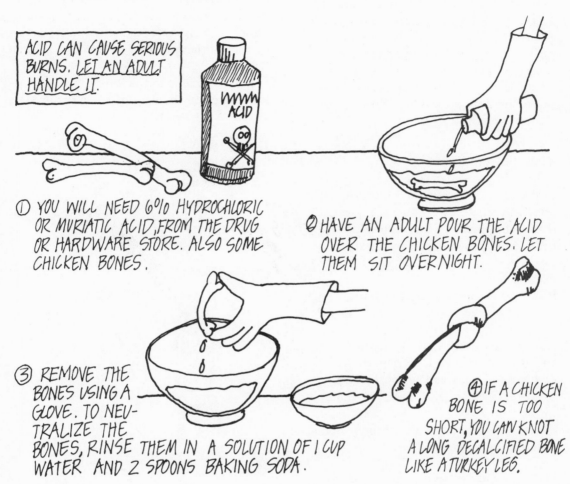

ACID CAN CAUSE SERIOUS BURNS. <u>LET AN ADULT HANDLE IT.</u>

① YOU WILL NEED 6% HYDROCHLORIC OR MURIATIC ACID, FROM THE DRUG OR HARDWARE STORE. ALSO SOME CHICKEN BONES.

② HAVE AN ADULT POUR THE ACID OVER THE CHICKEN BONES. LET THEM SIT OVERNIGHT.

③ REMOVE THE BONES USING A GLOVE. TO NEUTRALIZE THE BONES, RINSE THEM IN A SOLUTION OF 1 CUP WATER AND 2 SPOONS BAKING SODA.

④ IF A CHICKEN BONE IS TOO SHORT, YOU CAN KNOT A LONG DECALCIFIED BONE LIKE A TURKEY LEG.

Amazing Facts

— At birth humans have 300 bones. By the time adulthood is reached, the bones number 206, because some have fused together.

— Half of your bones are in your hands and feet.

— One person in twenty has an extra rib. This extra rib is three times more common in males.

— An old person often develops a slight curve in the spine. Right-handed people curve right, and left-handed people curve left.

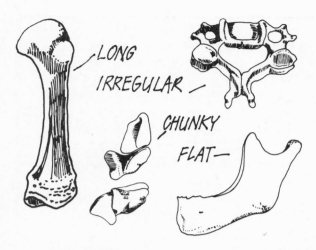

LONG
IRREGULAR
CHUNKY
FLAT

Kinds of Bones

The thighbone is not the only beautiful bone in your body. You have more than two hundred other bones, each beautifully fitted for its own particular place.

Bones come in some weird shapes. They fit into four basic groups.

Long bones are the skinny, hollow sort with the swollen ends. They are slightly curved so they can support more weight. Legs, arms, fingers, for example.

Short bones are the wide, chunky bones found in your feet and wrists.

Flat bones are platelike, like your ribs and shoulder blades.

Irregular bones are real weirdos that don't fit into any other group — bones like the vertebrae in your spine or the tiny bones inside your ear.

If you are interested in studying bones, you might ask for some old X-rays at your local hospital. If you break a bone of your own, ask the doctor if you can have the X-rays.

Joints

You can bend, swivel, stretch, snap, clench, pivot, and point. Your body can perform more than one kind of motion. Thus, your rigid bones are connected by more than one kind of joint.

Some man-made joints look like the following. In the case of the wrist and ankle joint there is no man-made equal.

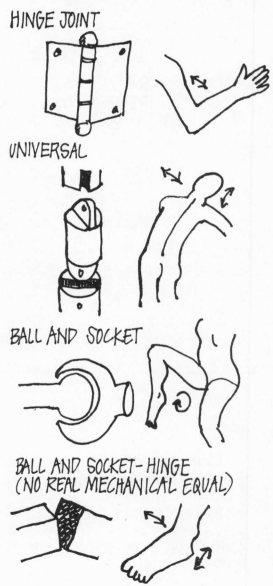

HINGE JOINT

UNIVERSAL

BALL AND SOCKET

BALL AND SOCKET-HINGE
(NO REAL MECHANICAL EQUAL)

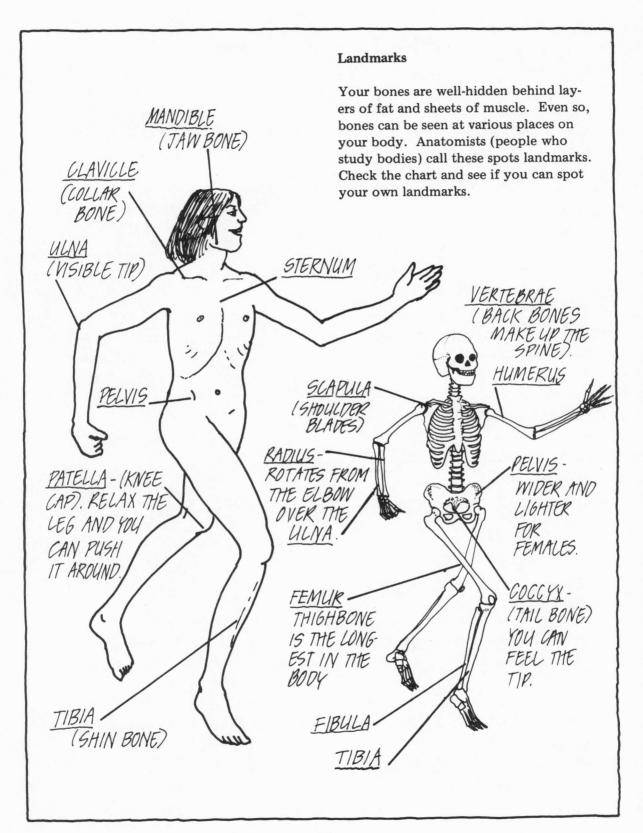

Landmarks

Your bones are well-hidden behind layers of fat and sheets of muscle. Even so, bones can be seen at various places on your body. Anatomists (people who study bodies) call these spots landmarks. Check the chart and see if you can spot your own landmarks.

MANDIBLE (JAW BONE)

CLAVICLE (COLLAR BONE)

ULNA (VISIBLE TIP)

STERNUM

VERTEBRAE (BACK BONES MAKE UP THE SPINE).

HUMERUS

SCAPULA (SHOULDER BLADES)

PELVIS

RADIUS- ROTATES FROM THE ELBOW OVER THE ULNA.

PELVIS- WIDER AND LIGHTER FOR FEMALES.

PATELLA - (KNEE CAP). RELAX THE LEG AND YOU CAN PUSH IT AROUND.

FEMUR THIGHBONE IS THE LONGEST IN THE BODY

COCCYX- (TAIL BONE) YOU CAN FEEL THE TIP.

TIBIA (SHIN BONE)

FIBULA

TIBIA

Cutting Up

Dissecting is not standing in a pool of blood hacking up dead or half-dead things. Any dissector worth a scalpel cuts only as a last resort, letting the probe separate delicate tissues. Dissection is neat, careful work. You can purchase dissecting tools from a biological supply house. Check your phone book to see if there is one in your town. Or you can make your own with stuff from around the house.

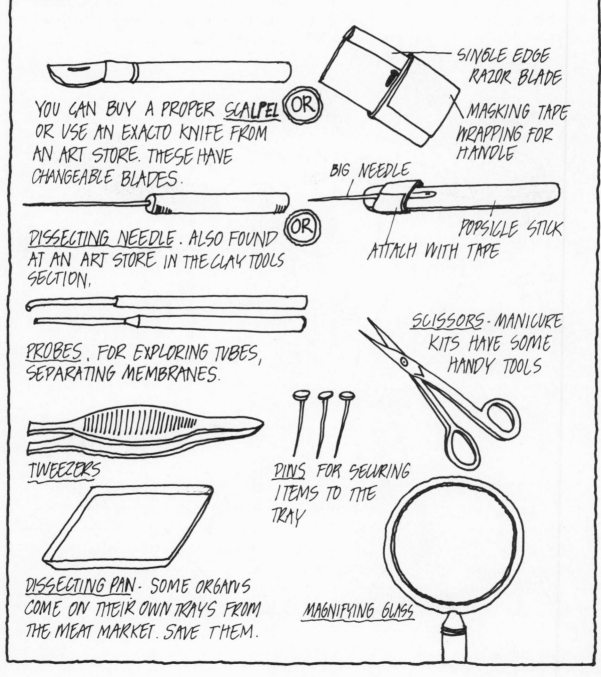

YOU CAN BUY A PROPER SCALPEL OR OR USE AN EXACTO KNIFE FROM AN ART STORE. THESE HAVE CHANGEABLE BLADES.

SINGLE EDGE RAZOR BLADE

MASKING TAPE WRAPPING FOR HANDLE

BIG NEEDLE

DISSECTING NEEDLE. ALSO FOUND OR AT AN ART STORE IN THE CLAY TOOLS SECTION.

POPSICLE STICK

ATTACH WITH TAPE

PROBES. FOR EXPLORING TUBES, SEPARATING MEMBRANES.

SCISSORS. MANICURE KITS HAVE SOME HANDY TOOLS

TWEEZERS

PINS FOR SECURING ITEMS TO THE TRAY

DISSECTING PAN. SOME ORGANS COME ON THEIR OWN TRAYS FROM THE MEAT MARKET. SAVE THEM.

MAGNIFYING GLASS

Inside a Long Bone Ask your butcher for soup bones. Tell him you are interested in studying bones. Try to get a cylindrical bone like the shin. Ask him to saw it lengthwise so you can look inside. If you want to do a joint dissection, ask for some beef knuckles. Pick one with the most tissue left on it. You can freeze it if you don't want to use it right away.

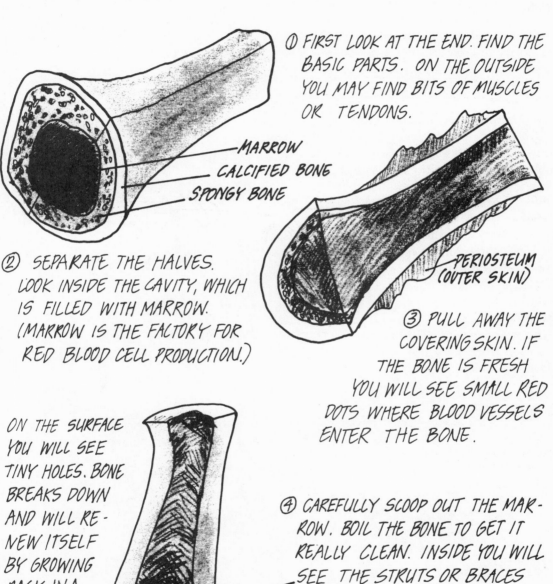

① FIRST LOOK AT THE END. FIND THE BASIC PARTS. ON THE OUTSIDE YOU MAY FIND BITS OF MUSCLES OR TENDONS.

MARROW
CALCIFIED BONE
SPONGY BONE

PERIOSTEUM (OUTER SKIN)

② SEPARATE THE HALVES. LOOK INSIDE THE CAVITY, WHICH IS FILLED WITH MARROW. (MARROW IS THE FACTORY FOR RED BLOOD CELL PRODUCTION.)

③ PULL AWAY THE COVERING SKIN. IF THE BONE IS FRESH YOU WILL SEE SMALL RED DOTS WHERE BLOOD VESSELS ENTER THE BONE.

ON THE SURFACE YOU WILL SEE TINY HOLES. BONE BREAKS DOWN AND WILL RENEW ITSELF BY GROWING BACK IN A CONSTANT CYCLE.

④ CAREFULLY SCOOP OUT THE MARROW. BOIL THE BONE TO GET IT REALLY CLEAN. INSIDE YOU WILL SEE THE STRUTS OR BRACES THAT GROW ALONG LINES OF STRESS.

Body Plan

Humans belong to a group in the animal kingdom called *vertebrates* (VER tah brets). To belong to this group you must have a backbone. This includes fishes, birds, frogs, and mammals. Even so, it is a rather exclusive club. The large majority of creatures fall into other groups which we, often snobbily, call "spineless."

The first members of the vertebrate group grew up in the ancient oceans, about 300 million years ago. Their column of bones gave their muscles better support. This made them faster swimming, more successful fish.

Gradually, over millions of years, their bodies changed and began to better fit their environment. These gradual changes over generations are called evolution.

This is how scientists think vertebrates evolved from bony fish to two-legged land mammals:

LIZARD — TOUGH SKIN FOR DRY CLIMATE

DEVELOPED LEGS SET WIDE FOR WALKING

INSECTIVORES — WARM BLOODED

FUR COVER FOR SAVING HEAT

LEMUR — EYES POSITIONED IN FRONT

LONGER LIMBS FOR FASTER TRAVEL

HIGHER PRIMATES

HAVE MUCH IN COMMON. HUMAN POSTURE ALLOWS FOR EXTENSIVE USE OF THE HANDS.

BONY FISH

LOBE FINS BECAME STUBBY LEGS FOR LAND USE.

AMPHIBIAN

REAL LEGS FOR MOVING IN AND OUT OF WATER

LUNGS FOR BREATHING AIR

TWO LEG POSTURE

Primate

Certain vertebrates have made some further adjustments to their body plans, putting them in a class by themselves. They are called primates. Their special features include:

— Lengthened fingers and toes, with flat nails.

—Opposable thumbs.

— Eyes positioned in front for 3-D vision.

— Big brain and brain case.

— And something only humans have developed — the ability to walk on two limbs.

People who study evolution think these changes in the primate form were related to each other. Opposable thumbs and 3-D vision were perhaps the result of a swinging life in the trees. When primates stopped resting on their knuckles and began to spend more time on their feet, their hands were suddenly free for all sorts of activity. Enlarged brains were favored because they could coordinate and cope with all the new information and activity.

If you feel superior looking down on the rest of the vertebrate world from your elevated two-legged position, don't. Your back is still trying to adjust to this peculiar upright posture. A lot of human backaches are caused by poorly adjusted spines, spines that would be more comfortable in creatures on all fours.

Shrink Test You are not the same height all day long. Unbelievable? Try this test for yourself. Check your friends and relatives to see if you all shrink at the same rate.

1. CAREFULLY MEASURE YOUR HEIGHT WHEN YOU FIRST WAKE UP IN THE MORNING.

2. MEASURE AGAIN LATER. ANY CHANGE?

○ HOW LONG DOES IT TAKE TO SHRINK?
○ DO TALL PEOPLE SHRINK MORE OR LESS?
○ HOW ABOUT OLD PERSONS VS. YOUNG ONES?

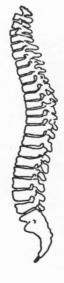

YOUR BACK BONE IS MADE OF SEPARATE BONES CALLED VERTEBRAE. SANDWICHED BETWEEN THE VERTEBRAE ARE SOFT CARTILAGE DISCS, WHICH ACT AS CUSHIONS. STANDING SQUEEZES OUT LIQUID IN THE DISCS WHICH ACCUMULATES AT NIGHT.

Basic Vertebrate Shape

Some people do not believe in the evolutionist theory. That's okay. Still, it doesn't change the fact that humans and horned toads have a lot in common. It may not be obvious at first, but if you do a bit of comparative anatomy, you will see that our body model and that of the toad have the same basic plan:

— Each has a main body stalk (trunk) with a supporting spine down the center back.

— Each has four limbs. (This is true for all vertebrates, even whales and snakes, who retain traces of them.)

— Each is bilaterally symmetrical. This means that if you draw a line along the center (spine), each side will be a mirror image of the other.

Great Thumbless Survival Test   It stands to reason: given certain equipment, you live a certain sort of life. All this is pretty much decided by the body you inhabit.

① HAVE SOMEONE TAPE YOUR THUMBS ACROSS YOUR PALM. LEAVE YOUR OTHER FINGERS FREE.

② PLAN TO STAY THUMBLESS FOR A LEAST ONE HOUR. DO ALL THE THINGS YOU NORMALLY DO. OR TRY IT ALL DAY. KEEP A RECORD.

WELL, WHAT GOOD ARE THEY? CAN YOU DRAW ANY CONCLUSIONS ABOUT THE KINDS OF ACTIVITIES THUMBLESS CREATURES CAN'T DO.

ACTIVITY	RESULTS
writing	
swimming	
eating	
base ball	
chin-ups	
marbles	
phoning	

Teeth

NIPPERS, CHOMPERS, GRINDERS

Until teeth were invented, animals were limited to a menu of things that would fit into their mouths. Teeth made it possible for small things to dine on larger things.

The first teeth appeared in the mouths of ancient sharklike fish. They were nothing more than fancy scales. All these teeth were pointed and alike. Sharks today have a mouth lined with four rows of rippers. As the front rows wear out, the back rows move forward to replace them.

Since those first beginnings, animals have developed an amazing array of teeth. Each creature has evolved a mouthful of tools best suited to its special life style.

Have you ever heard the expression "You are what you eat"? There is no place where it's truer than inside your mouth.

What Vore?

The question of how an animal makes its living is an open and shut case. Have a look at its mouth, or more precisely, at the teeth inside.

An animal that eats meat will have a lot of pointy teeth for ripping and tearing. This kind of animal is called a *carnivore* (CAR niv or).

An animal that eats grasses and leaves will have mostly flat teeth for grinding. This kind of animal is called a *herbivore* (HERB ih vor).

An animal that eats both kinds of food has an assorted set of teeth. This sort of animal is called an *omnivore* (OM ni vor).

What kind are you?

Casting   You can get a fairly good look at your teeth with mirrors. An even better way is to make a casting of your teeth with plaster of Paris. It's fun, and the results are wonderful.

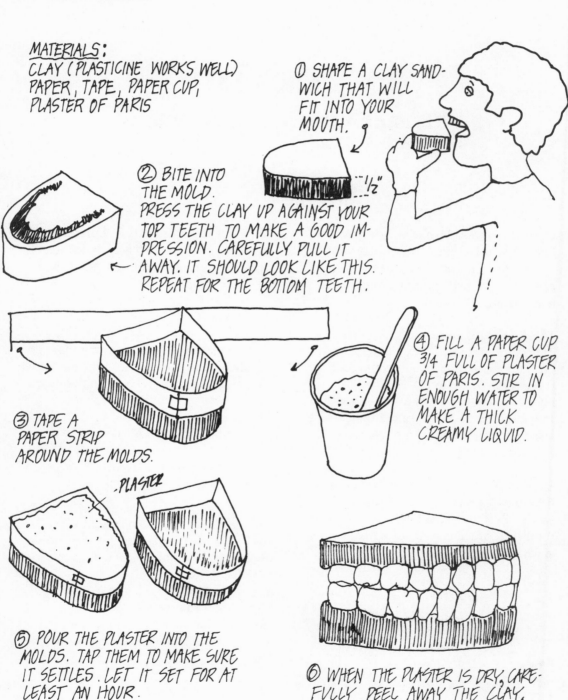

MATERIALS:
CLAY (PLASTICINE WORKS WELL)
PAPER, TAPE, PAPER CUP,
PLASTER OF PARIS

① SHAPE A CLAY SAND-WICH THAT WILL FIT INTO YOUR MOUTH.

···1/2"

② BITE INTO THE MOLD.
PRESS THE CLAY UP AGAINST YOUR TOP TEETH TO MAKE A GOOD IMPRESSION. CAREFULLY PULL IT AWAY. IT SHOULD LOOK LIKE THIS. REPEAT FOR THE BOTTOM TEETH.

③ TAPE A PAPER STRIP AROUND THE MOLDS.

④ FILL A PAPER CUP 3/4 FULL OF PLASTER OF PARIS. STIR IN ENOUGH WATER TO MAKE A THICK CREAMY LIQUID.

PLASTER

⑤ POUR THE PLASTER INTO THE MOLDS. TAP THEM TO MAKE SURE IT SETTLES. LET IT SET FOR AT LEAST AN HOUR.

⑥ WHEN THE PLASTER IS DRY, CAREFULLY PEEL AWAY THE CLAY.

32

Nippers, Rippers, Grinders Test How many kinds of teeth do you have? Why so many models for one mouth? Before you answer, you might try the following experiment.

PEANUT BRITTLE
BANANAS
BEEF JERKY
NUTS

CELERY

CHEESE
APPLE
CARROTS

GATHER UP SOME DIFFERENT KINDS OF FOODS. CHEW EACH ONE SLOWLY.
PAY ATTENTION AND COMPARE HOW YOUR TEETH TREAT EACH FOOD.

Something Missing?

Chances are that unless you are a big kid (over twenty-one) your teeth don't look quite like the cast on the opposite page.

That is because you are still losing baby teeth. Human animals get two sets of teeth. You grow one set to fit your child-size jaws. As your jaws grow, you slowly shed your baby teeth. A full set of adult teeth takes its place in your full-size adult jaws. Teeth can't grow. They are covered with a hard non-living coat of enamel which prevents further growth. They have no choice but to fall out to make way for their bigger replacements.

In fact, another name for baby teeth is *deciduous* (de CID you us). This is the same name given to trees that drop their autumn leaves. Deciduous means falling.

Open Wide

In the front you have big, flat, wedge-shaped teeth called *incisors* (in SIGH zors). They work much like scissors. The upper and lower teeth fit closely together like two blades. Open them up and close them around a bit of food. They nip out neat bites.

Around the corner are sharp pointy teeth called *canines* (KAY nines) or dog teeth. If you ever chewed meat off a bone, you know how they got their name.

Next come the *bicuspids* (bi CUSS pids). This word means having two points.

In the back are the flat *molars* (MOE lars). This word means millstone. The bicuspids and molars are both in the grinding department.

Tooth Dissection

If you have an old tooth around that the tooth fairy hasn't spirited away, you can crack it open to look at the parts.

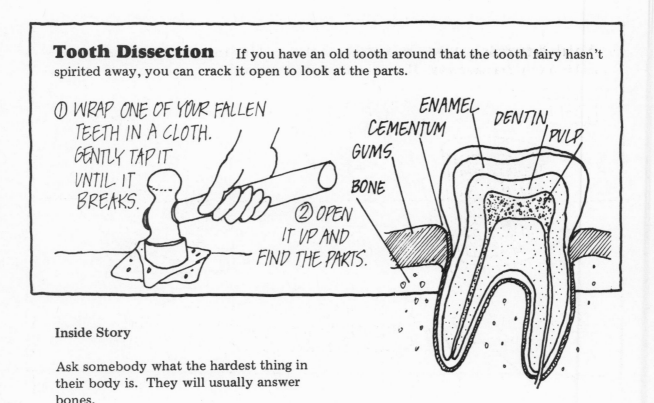

① WRAP ONE OF YOUR FALLEN TEETH IN A CLOTH. GENTLY TAP IT UNTIL IT BREAKS.

② OPEN IT UP AND FIND THE PARTS.

ENAMEL
CEMENTUM
DENTIN
PULP
GUMS
BONE

Inside Story

Ask somebody what the hardest thing in their body is. They will usually answer bones.

Well, it's not bones. The answer is teeth. Teeth are not bones, even though they look like them in many ways.

The inner part of the tooth is called the pulp. Like the inside of a bone it contains nerves and blood vessels. It is the living tooth.

Dentin is the next layer. It is similar to bone, but harder. Piano keys made from elephant tusks are almost pure dentin.

Enamel is the tough outer coat. It is 98% mineral material. It is like rock in its hardness and structure. It is inactive and once damaged, can't repair itself.

Cementum (see MENT um) is the outer coating of the tooth's roots. Each tooth snuggles in its own space in the jaw bone. Cementum holds it firmly in place.

Cavities Mean Holes

Tooth enamel is tough stuff, but not indestructible. The number one enemy of enamel is acid. Acid eats enamel. Hardly anyone eats pure acid, but lots of people get cavities. Just how does acid get into your mouth?

Mouths harbor many kinds of bacteria (microcreatures). In fact your mouth is the most contaminated spot you've got. Think about that for a minute.

Some of this microlife eats the same food you do — bits of bread, caramel candy, spaghetti. That is why bacteria are hanging out inside your mouth in the first place. As they break down food they produce acid. Acid can attack the tooth enamel, leaving holes and the living tooth wide open to infection.

Acid Attack

Eggshells are similar in their makeup to teeth. Both react to acid in a very dramatic way. Here is how to test an eggshell.

TEST I

① LET AN EGG SOAK OVER NIGHT IN ACID.
② REMOVE THE EGG.

TEST II

IS SODA POP ACID ENOUGH TO EAT TEETH?

① DROP A TOOTH INTO YOUR FAVORITE SOFT DRINK. DATE THE BOTTLE.
② CHECK THE TOOTH TWICE A WEEK. RETURN IT TO THE BOTTLE.

Counterattack

Do you ever not brush your teeth for a while? Soon your teeth begin to feel like moss is growing on them. That mossy feeling is caused by *plaque* (PLAK).

Plaque is a mixture of bits of food, saliva, and bacteria. It is bad news for a tooth to be covered by a lot of acid-making bacteria having their lunch.

At first the plaque is soft and invisible. If it is allowed to stay on a tooth, it turns into a yellow, crusty scum called tartar. Tartar is difficult to remove. The dentist scrapes it away when you have your teeth cleaned.

The old toothbrush routine is important. It knocks the plaque off before bacteria can gang up and harm your teeth, and before plaque can harden into tartar.

Red Alert   There is a way to make plaque visible. You need something called disclosing tablets. They don't taste bad and leave you with a terrific red smile. Dentists use them to find plaque deposits. You can buy them at the drug store, or ask your dentist for some.

① CHEW A TABLET. SWISH IT AROUND IN YOUR MOUTH FOR 30 SECONDS. RINSE.

DISCLOSING TABLET

WATER

② SHOCKING, ISN'T IT? ALL THOSE RED SPOTS ARE PLAQUE. SPOTS WHERE YOUR TOOTH BRUSH ISN'T GOING. NOW BRUSH.

Golden Tooth Rule

Leaving bits of food in your mouth is tooth murder. Some foods are worse than others. You know the worst: sticky, gooey sweets and acid foods with sugar. On the other hand, there are some foods that are tooth cleaners.

Here is a list of enamel assassins:

Imitation fruit juice
Soda pop
Sticky candy
White bread
Dried fruit (like raisins)
Gum
Macaroni

And here are some self-cleaners:

Carrots
Apples
Pickles
Plums
Melons
Celery
Tomatoes

WHATEVER LEAVES YOUR MOUTH SLICK AND SHINEY IS GOOD FOR TEETH!

Muscles
YOUR MIGHTY MOVERS

Think of motion and you think of Billie Jean King hitting a backhand, or O. J. Simpson streaking for a touchdown.

Muscles are responsible for your body's every move. Besides making touchdowns, muscles keep your tongue wagging, your gut from sagging, your heart pounding, your lungs pumping. Muscles keep your throat clear and your food moving along.

Muscles are more than movers. In the process of all their work, they make much of the heat that keeps you warm.

System of Squeezers

Your body is able to bend, reach, twist, lift, flip, leap, and more.

The amazing thing is that *all* this activity results from just one muscle action. That's right, muscles can perform just one single motion. A muscle can make itself shorter — it can contract. When it is not doing that, it relaxes.

Do not underestimate this seemingly simple action. Many muscle scientists have spent many years studying this problem. What they do know is that a muscle receives an electric command from the brain through the nerves. This triggers a lightning-quick change of chemical fuel which causes the muscle to contract. Many of the details of how this happens are still a mystery that a lot of scientists would give their biceps to solve.

Muscle Teams

Flex your biceps. You can feel the muscle contract. You can watch it get that big bulgy look that he-man types are so proud of.

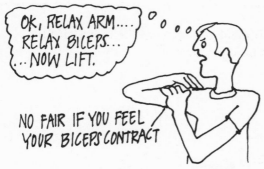

Now relax your arm in this position.

Try to get your arm out of this position using *only* your biceps. This will take some concentration.

If you did it, you cheated. Muscles can only contract. Contracting the biceps harder will only bring the forearm closer. There is no way in the world you can get the arm out of that position by squeezing the biceps.

What you need is a muscle on the other side that can contract and produce a motion in the opposite direction. You have just such a muscle. (Lift your forearm away from your shoulder and notice where the muscle contraction occurs.)

Your muscles work in teams. This is true all over your body. Every set of muscles has at least one opposing set so your movements can be reversed. These opposing teams also help to coordinate your motions by acting as brakes while the others are moving.

You can feel your muscles at work flexing and relaxing. Take a survey with your fingers. Do some movements and find the muscle teams responsible.

Model Arm

You can make a rather nice model arm that will help explain the workings of muscle teams. It will also look splendid on your wall.

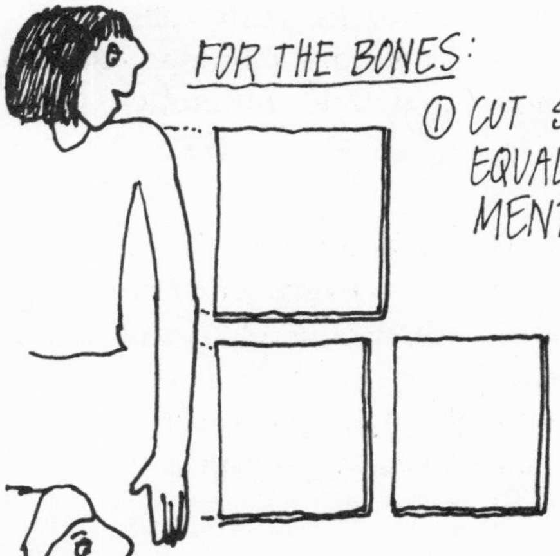

FOR THE BONES:

① CUT SOME CARDBOARD SQUARES EQUAL TO YOUR ARM MEASUREMENTS (IN LENGTH).

② ROLL THEM TIGHTLY. BIND THE ENDS WITH TAPE. LABEL THEM.

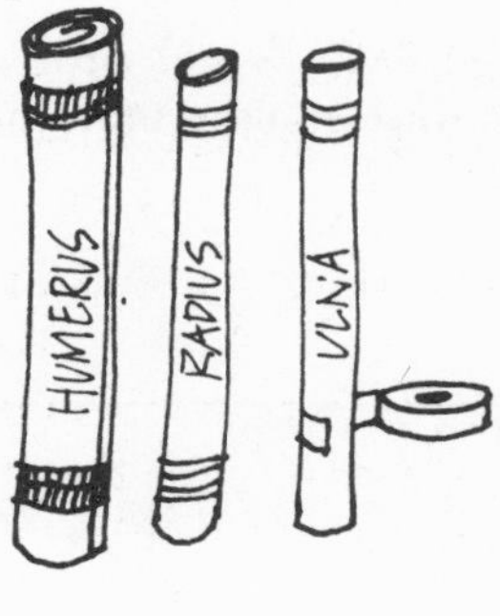

HUMERUS RADIUS ULNA

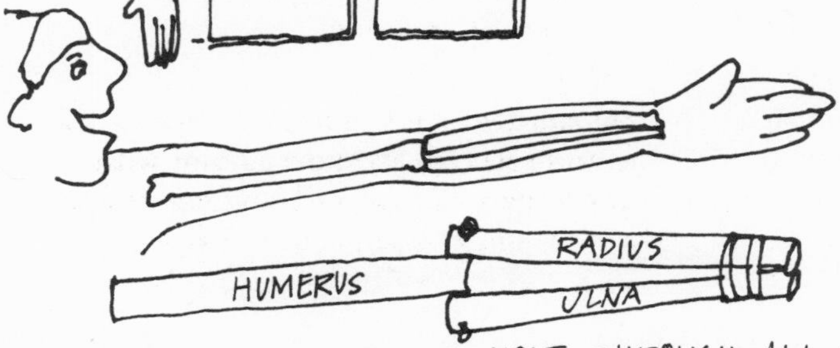

HUMERUS RADIUS ULNA

FOR THE JOINT: MAKE A HOLE THROUGH ALL THREE BONES WITH SOMETHING SHARP. UNBEND A PAPER CLIP. THREAD IT THROUGH THE HOLES. LOOP THE ENDS.

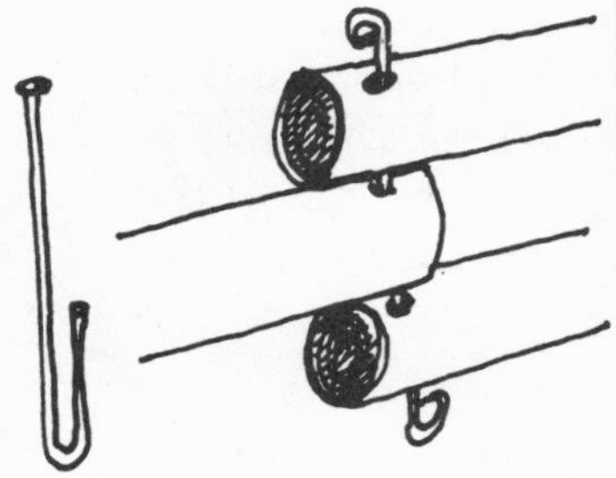

FOR THE MUSCLES: SLIGHTLY INFLATE TWO LONG BALLOONS. TIE KNOTS IN BOTH ENDS.

① TIE ON THE BALLOON MUSCLES. FIRST THE BICEPS.  THEN THE TRICEPS.

REMEMBER THAT THIS ARM HAS ONLY TWO MUSCLES. A REAL ONE HAS MANY.

② WHAT HAPPENS WHEN THE BICEPS CONTRACTS? (GETS FATTER?)

Inside a Muscle

Muscles are made up of long skinny cells. These cells group together and form long strands called *fibrils* (FIE brills). Groups of fibrils form a muscle bundle. A lot of bundles make up a muscle group, like the biceps.

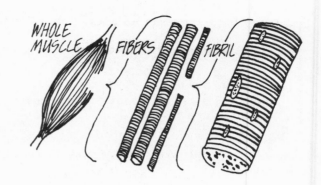

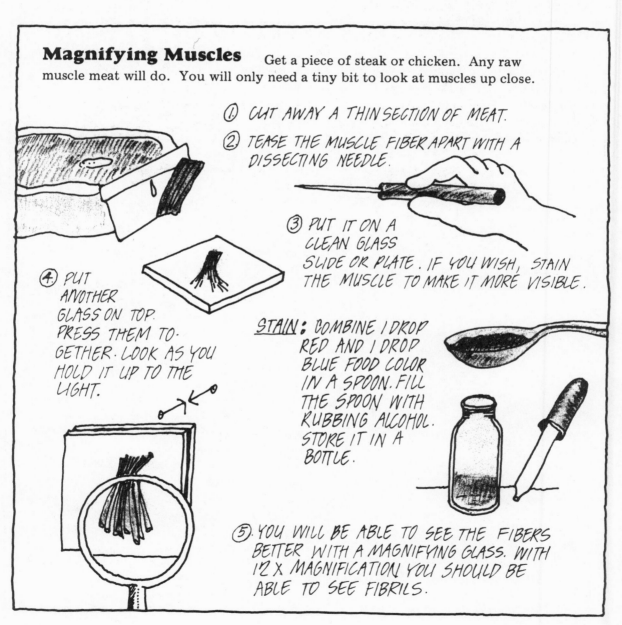

Magnifying Muscles

Get a piece of steak or chicken. Any raw muscle meat will do. You will only need a tiny bit to look at muscles up close.

① CUT AWAY A THIN SECTION OF MEAT.

② TEASE THE MUSCLE FIBER APART WITH A DISSECTING NEEDLE.

③ PUT IT ON A CLEAN GLASS SLIDE OR PLATE. IF YOU WISH, STAIN THE MUSCLE TO MAKE IT MORE VISIBLE.

STAIN: COMBINE 1 DROP RED AND 1 DROP BLUE FOOD COLOR IN A SPOON. FILL THE SPOON WITH RUBBING ALCOHOL. STORE IT IN A BOTTLE.

④ PUT ANOTHER GLASS ON TOP. PRESS THEM TOGETHER. LOOK AS YOU HOLD IT UP TO THE LIGHT.

⑤ YOU WILL BE ABLE TO SEE THE FIBERS BETTER WITH A MAGNIFYING GLASS. WITH 12 X MAGNIFICATION YOU SHOULD BE ABLE TO SEE FIBRILS.

40

Muscle Landmarks

There are more than six hundred muscle groups in the human body. Like bones, the muscles that make an appearance on the body's surface are called landmarks. Here is a short tour of your landmark muscles.

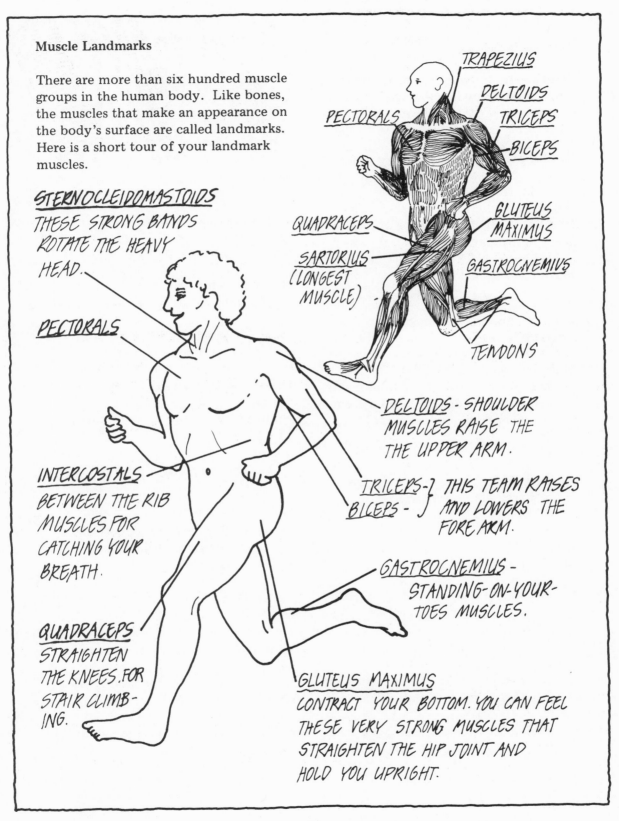

STERNOCLEIDOMASTOIDS
THESE STRONG BANDS ROTATE THE HEAVY HEAD.

PECTORALS

INTERCOSTALS
BETWEEN THE RIB MUSCLES FOR CATCHING YOUR BREATH.

QUADRACEPS
STRAIGHTEN THE KNEES. FOR STAIR CLIMBING.

TRAPEZIUS
DELTOIDS
TRICEPS
BICEPS
PECTORALS
GLUTEUS MAXIMUS
QUADRACEPS
SARTORIUS (LONGEST MUSCLE)
GASTROCNEMIUS
TENDONS

DELTOIDS - SHOULDER MUSCLES RAISE THE THE UPPER ARM.

TRICEPS -⎤ THIS TEAM RAISES
BICEPS - ⎦ AND LOWERS THE FORE ARM.

GASTROCNEMIUS - STANDING-ON-YOUR-TOES MUSCLES.

GLUTEUS MAXIMUS
CONTRACT YOUR BOTTOM. YOU CAN FEEL THESE VERY STRONG MUSCLES THAT STRAIGHTEN THE HIP JOINT AND HOLD YOU UPRIGHT.

Three Kinds of Muscles

You have three sorts of muscles. Altogether they make up about one half of your body.

Skeletal muscles are the muscles that move your bones around, like your biceps. But they move other parts of you as well, like your eyes. These muscles are made up of straight strips of muscle fiber lying side by side. They are voluntary muscles. That is, they operate on command from your brain.

A smooth muscle is put together a little differently. It works automatically, at a slow, more continuous pace than a skeletal muscle. Smooth muscle is in charge of the body's internal movements, like pumping food around in your stomach or squeezing blood into your blood vessels.

Cardiac is a special name given to the strong muscles in your heart.

All or Nothing

A single muscle fiber can either contract or remain relaxed. There is no half way for a muscle.

In a way, it's the same for a light. A light is either on or off. There is no such thing as a light that is sort of on.

For muscles this doesn't seem quite true. It seems your arm muscles have to be a lot more "on" to lift a bagful of groceries than they do to lift a glass of milk.

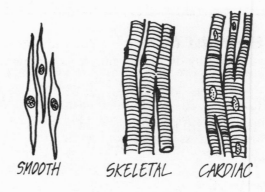

SMOOTH   SKELETAL   CARDIAC

Remember, what you call a muscle is really a mass of muscle fibers. When you lift a glass of milk, you contract only a few fibers. However, lifting your bicycle, or a twenty-gallon can of chicken soup might contract every fiber you have.

When sustained muscle power is needed, muscle fibers take turns contracting and relaxing. No one fiber can contract for longer than a fraction of a second. A muscle group can remain contracted for a much longer time because individual fibers take turns twitching.

Tone

Muscles spend their time slightly contracted. They constantly exercise themselves. So, when they are called into action, they are warmed up and ready to work on short notice. This continuous contraction of the muscles of the body is called muscle tone.

When a person is nervous, his muscles will have a great deal of muscle tone. He will jump at the slightest noise, because his muscles are keyed up and ready to respond. A relaxed person retains a good deal of muscle tone, but not nearly so much as a nervous person. During sleep the muscles are allowed to relax almost completely, and retain very little tone.

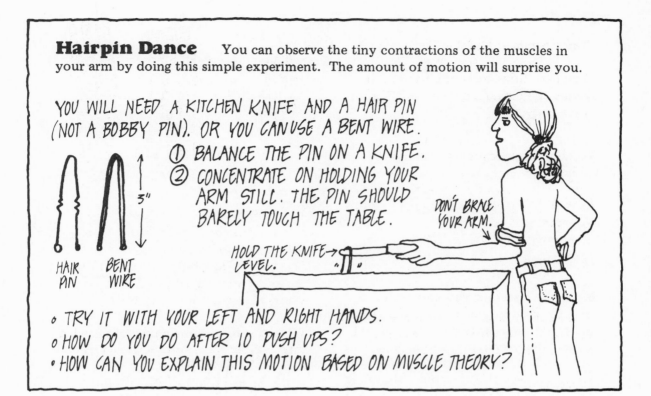

Hairpin Dance You can observe the tiny contractions of the muscles in your arm by doing this simple experiment. The amount of motion will surprise you.

YOU WILL NEED A KITCHEN KNIFE AND A HAIR PIN (NOT A BOBBY PIN). OR YOU CAN USE A BENT WIRE.
① BALANCE THE PIN ON A KNIFE.
② CONCENTRATE ON HOLDING YOUR ARM STILL. THE PIN SHOULD BARELY TOUCH THE TABLE.

3"

HAIR PIN   BENT WIRE

DON'T BRACE YOUR ARM.

HOLD THE KNIFE→ LEVEL.

o TRY IT WITH YOUR LEFT AND RIGHT HANDS.
o HOW DO YOU DO AFTER 10 PUSH UPS?
• HOW CAN YOU EXPLAIN THIS MOTION BASED ON MUSCLE THEORY?

Tired Muscles

You can run only so many blocks before your legs feel like rubber. Your muscles work well up to a point, until tiredness forces you to rest them. Just what is this point of tiredness?

Muscle fiber can contract many times a second. When doing this, a muscle quickly uses up its stored fuel. Then more nutrients and oxygen are resupplied to it by the blood. Your heart pounds and you pant, trying to gulp in as much oxygen as fast as you can. Sometimes you can't do it fast enough. (The body is able to make a little muscle energy without oxygen. It's not much, to be sure, but that little extra can be important when being chased by a pack of wild boars.)

Everything has a price. When the body produces that extra little energy without oxygen, a chemical collects in the muscles called lactic acid. The muscles don't like lactic acid hanging around because it means they have a harder and harder time contracting. Soon they slow down, exhausted, and refuse to work any more until they have had a period of relaxation. This is when you put down the load you're carrying, or stop running or whatever it is you've been doing. Working your muscles until they scream murder causes you to borrow heavily on your body's oxygen supply. You are in debt.

In order to get rid of that lactic acid in your muscles, you need oxygen. So you keep panting, and your heart keeps pounding, until your oxygen debt has been repaid.

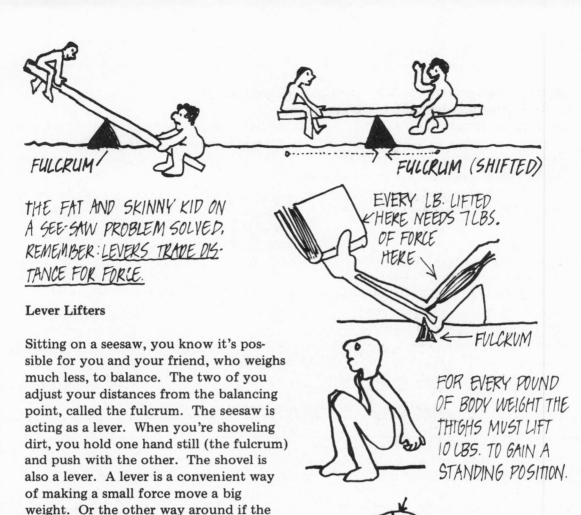

FULCRUM

FULCRUM (SHIFTED)

THE FAT AND SKINNY KID ON A SEE-SAW PROBLEM SOLVED. REMEMBER: <u>LEVERS TRADE DISTANCE FOR FORCE.</u>

EVERY LB. LIFTED HERE NEEDS 7 LBS. OF FORCE HERE

FULCRUM

Lever Lifters

Sitting on a seesaw, you know it's possible for you and your friend, who weighs much less, to balance. The two of you adjust your distances from the balancing point, called the fulcrum. The seesaw is acting as a lever. When you're shoveling dirt, you hold one hand still (the fulcrum) and push with the other. The shovel is also a lever. A lever is a convenient way of making a small force move a big weight. Or the other way around if the weight is hard to get at.

Your body has arranged its muscles so that they act as levers for moving your bones and the rest of you. Rest your forearm flat on a table, put a dictionary in your hand, and then raise it, keeping your elbow touching the table. If the dictionary weighs four pounds, the biceps muscle in your arm provides about twenty-eight pounds of force so that you can raise it. Your arm acts as a lever, with your elbow as fulcrum.

Every body movement you make involves muscles moving bones that act as levers. The arrangements often involve levers moving levers, and the forces produced by your muscles can be amazingly great.

FOR EVERY POUND OF BODY WEIGHT THE THIGHS MUST LIFT 10 LBS. TO GAIN A STANDING POSITION.

LIFTING 50 LBS WITH A ROUND BACK CAN PUT 800 LBS. STRAIN ON THE LOWER SPINE. (USE BENT KNEES).

Muscles You Forgot You Had

Muscles will shrink up and become useless if they don't get exercised. This can happen over a short period of time, for instance, if you stop using a leg because it is broken. Muscles can also become useless over generations, as in the case of the flight muscles of penguins. This process is called *atrophy* (A tro fee).

So what, you are thinking, dumb birds who use their wings for flippers deserve all the atrophy they get. Well, you have some yourself. Just there, behind your ears.

Humans have ear-wiggling muscles. However, most humans have lost the ability to use them. Once, a flip of the earlobe might have meant the difference between hearing or missing an approaching creature stalking some lunch.

How about you? Can you wiggle yours?

Face Flexing

In trying to get your ears to move, your forehead wrinkled, eyebrows flew up, eyes widened, and your jaws tightened.

These lifts and twitches are a special talent of humans. Most animal faces are immobile. Have you ever seen a lion laugh, or a snake smile?

Human faces are laced with lots of small muscles. You don't pay much attention to your own face muscles. However, they do a lot of communicating. For instance, the way your dad lifts or drops the corners of his mouth can mean the difference in a week's allowance.

Calisthenics for Your Face

Here are some exercises to try out on your face. They are fun to do and more fun to watch. Learning how to control your face might come in handy if you decide to take up acting or poker.

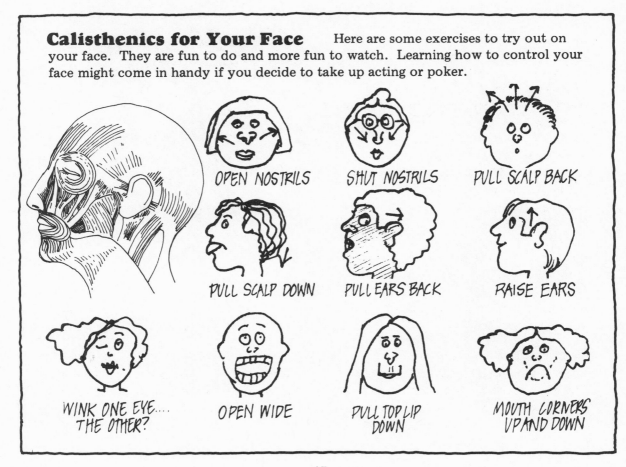

OPEN NOSTRILS SHUT NOSTRILS PULL SCALP BACK

PULL SCALP DOWN PULL EARS BACK RAISE EARS

WINK ONE EYE.... THE OTHER? OPEN WIDE PULL TOP LIP DOWN MOUTH CORNERS UP AND DOWN

Muscle, Tendon, Joint Dissection

Cutting apart a chicken leg is a good way to learn about muscle groups and how they are attached to the bone. It will also give you a good look at a joint. So, you might want to save this project until you have read up on joints in the section on bones. You will need a chicken drumstick and thigh that are still attached to each other.

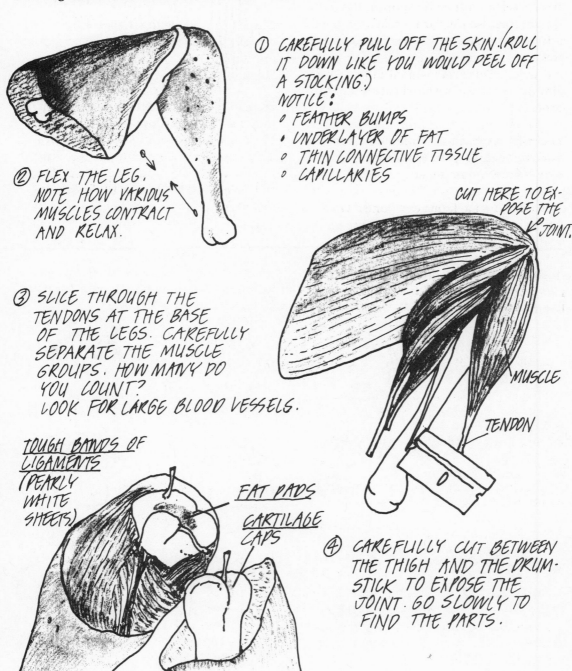

① CAREFULLY PULL OFF THE SKIN. (ROLL IT DOWN LIKE YOU WOULD PEEL OFF A STOCKING.)
NOTICE:
o FEATHER BUMPS
• UNDERLAYER OF FAT
o THIN CONNECTIVE TISSUE
o CAPILLARIES

② FLEX THE LEG. NOTE HOW VARIOUS MUSCLES CONTRACT AND RELAX.

③ SLICE THROUGH THE TENDONS AT THE BASE OF THE LEGS. CAREFULLY SEPARATE THE MUSCLE GROUPS. HOW MANY DO YOU COUNT?
LOOK FOR LARGE BLOOD VESSELS.

CUT HERE TO EXPOSE THE JOINT.

MUSCLE

TENDON

TOUGH BANDS OF LIGAMENTS (PEARLY WHITE SHEETS)

FAT PADS

CARTILAGE CAPS

④ CAREFULLY CUT BETWEEN THE THIGH AND THE DRUMSTICK TO EXPOSE THE JOINT. GO SLOWLY TO FIND THE PARTS.

The Ties That Bind

Tendons are the ties that bind muscles to your bones. These tough, cordlike bands of tissue concentrate the full force of a muscle at a specific spot on the bone. Tendons also allow for muscle action at a distance. Your fingers are primarily powered by muscles far off in your palm and wrist. This arrangement allows your slim fingers to be both delicate and strong.

You can watch these tendon cords at work by making your hand into a claw. Wiggle your index finger and watch the tendon move over your knuckle and slide over the back of your hand. Give it a feel. Like thick cords, tendons are made of a very strong, fibrous material. Lab tests have shown that tendons have stood stresses up to nine tons per square inch. In fact, bones will usually break before tendons will tear.

Human Rubber Band

Some people can bend over and put the backs of their hands flat on the floor.

Some people can bend over and touch their toes.

And then there are some people who can barely bend over.

Being able to bend and stretch is called flexibility. Flexibility is the ability to flex tendons.

Chances are if you are young you are still fairly flexible. But even kids have varying amounts of flexibility. Just because you have it one place doesn't mean you will have it another.

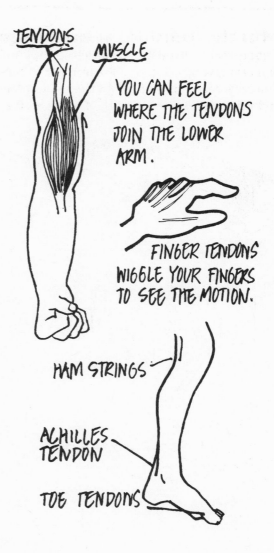

TENDONS
MUSCLE

YOU CAN FEEL WHERE THE TENDONS JOIN THE LOWER ARM.

FINGER TENDONS WIGGLE YOUR FINGERS TO SEE THE MOTION.

HAM STRINGS

ACHILLES TENDON

TOE TENDONS

Amazing Facts

— There are more than 600 muscles in the human body.

— If all the muscles in the body could pull in one direction in one mighty heave, the force would equal 25 tons.

— The average person's muscles do daily work amounting to loading 24,000 pounds onto a four-foot-high shelf. Think about that over a lifetime.

Flexercise

Here are some ways to test your flexibility. Try these stretches with a friend so you can compare. Before you he-men in the audience flip the page, you should know that males tend to be less flexible than females. While you may not be interested in joining the circus or the ballet, keeping flexible is good for your body. You can encourage those tight spots with a little daily stretching.

INSTEP – EXTEND TOE, CAN YOU GET A STRAIGHT LINE? / FLEX TO RAISE HEEL.

INSIDE THIGHS — PULL HEEL CLOSE TO HIP.

TOE TURN OUT — TRY TO TOUCH FLOOR.

KNEE – HOW FAR CAN YOU BEND THE KNEE? (HEEL STAYS ON THE FLOOR)

UPPER THIGHS — LEAN BACK KEEP BODY STRAIGHT.

HIP – PULL THE LEG TOWARD THE NOSE. THEN STRETCH OUT TO THE SIDE. (BOTH SIDES)

SPINE – CAN YOU TOUGH YOUR KNEES TO THE FLOOR?

SPINE · CAN YOU TOUCH YOUR HEAD AND TOES?

ARMS · STEP THROUGH BROOM. THEN UP AND OVER.. DON'T LET GO.

HAND CLASP – CAN YOU TOUCH OR JUST SHAKE? SHIFT POSITIONS.

Heart
THE DOUBLE-BARRELED PUMPER

Internal Organic Soup — Life's Blood

Once upon the earliest times, the first creatures floated in oceans that both nourished and covered them. These were tiny bloodless beings.

As they grew in size and complexity over the ages, they needed more forceful ways of sending the nourishing fluids to their cells. So these creatures invented a thing to pump fluid throughout their hungry bodies. This pumper is called a heart. The nourishing sealike fluid eventually became blood.

Hollow Muscle

Ask anyone what their strongest muscle is. You will receive a variety of answers, and hardly anyone will answer the heart.

But tell them, and hardly anyone will dispute the fact that their hard-working heart must be made of tough stuff.

After all, it must perform the job of pumping blood day and night for a lifetime.

Two-Barreled Ticker

You can think of your heart as two pumps working side by side.

On your right side (pretend you are wearing the drawing on page 52) is the heart that pumps blood to your lungs, where it picks up oxygen.

On your left side is the heart that pumps this oxygen-soaked blood out to your body.

Both pumps are divided into two spaces called chambers. So your heart is actually a two-barreled, four-chambered pumper. The two sides do not work independently. They are precisely timed as a team to make the best use of their pumping power. This is a very efficient system, which is much improved over the simple hearts belonging to slugs and sea anemones.

Tennis Ball Squeeze Try to do a heart's work with your hand. Test the ease with which you can squeeze, and get a grasp on the power of this mighty muscle.

GIVE IT A GOOD SQUEEZE.

① THE FORCE NEEDED TO SQUEEZE A TENNIS BALL IS SIMILAR TO THE FORCE NEEDED TO SQUEEZE BLOOD OUT OF THE HEART.

② IF YOU SQUEEZE 70 X A MINUTE (THE NORMAL PULSE), YOU WILL GET A FIRST HAND IDEA OF HOW HARD YOUR HEART WORKS.

Listen In

As your heart pumps, it makes a variety of clicks and thumps. Each sound has a special meaning if you know how to listen in.

First you need to find the place where the pulse is strongest. Many people think their hearts are on the left side. That's not exactly true. The heart is hung in the center of the chest between your lungs, just under your breastbone.

It is tipped a little to one side. This is where the confusion arises. The tip sticks out and taps against the left side of the chest. This is the spot where it is most easily felt and heard.

(Note: You may have a hard time hearing heart sounds. Be patient. Move your stethoscope. Get rid of as much background noise as you can. If you still have problems, skip rope or tap dance first for a minute.)

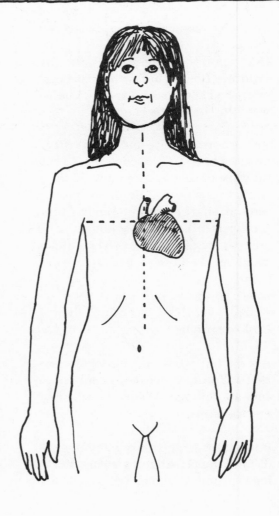

Stethoscope

The first stethoscope was invented by a doctor in 1819. It was nothing more than a hollow tube. However, it was an improvement over the old ear-on-the-chest method — at least in some cases. You can make one with a paper tube or a sheet of rolled-up writing paper. You can also make a more modern version with a rubber tube and a funnel. Here's how:

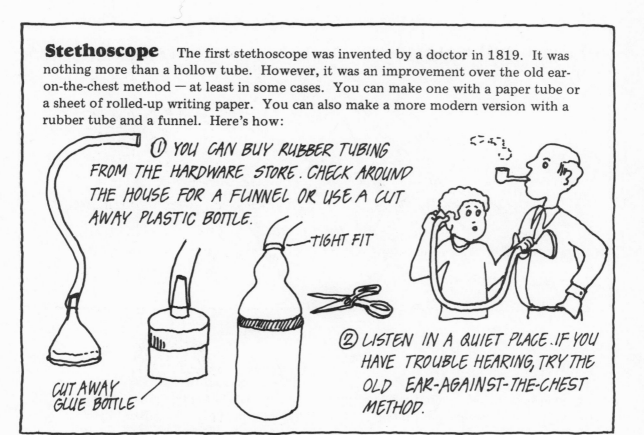

① YOU CAN BUY RUBBER TUBING FROM THE HARDWARE STORE. CHECK AROUND THE HOUSE FOR A FUNNEL OR USE A CUT AWAY PLASTIC BOTTLE.

TIGHT FIT

CUT AWAY GLUE BOTTLE

② LISTEN IN A QUIET PLACE. IF YOU HAVE TROUBLE HEARING, TRY THE OLD EAR-AGAINST-THE-CHEST METHOD.

Heart Sounds

You will hear two sounds during every heartbeat. Some people call them pitty-pat sounds. Doctors call them lub-dub noises.

These are the sounds of the heart valves as they click open and shut. The sound goes something like this: lub-DUB — lub-DUB — lub-DUB —

Lub is the sound of the *triscupid* (tri CUS pid) and *mitral* (MY tral) heart valves shutting. (Those are the ones on the top chambers.)

Then a pause. (Now the top chambers relax.)

Dub is the sound of the *semilunar* (sem ee LU nar) heart valves closing. These heart valves shut off the big vessels leaving the heart.

Then a longer pause.

lub-DUB — lub-DUB

Murmur

Sometimes the clear clicking noises of the heartbeat may sound a little blurred. Something like lubb-shhb DUB, or lubb-DUB rumble. This means the valves aren't working properly, and there is some leakage. This is called a murmur, and is very rare.

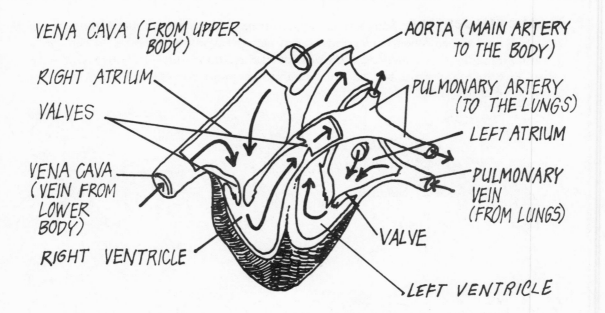

VENA CAVA (FROM UPPER BODY)

RIGHT ATRIUM

VALVES

VENA CAVA (VEIN FROM LOWER BODY)

RIGHT VENTRICLE

AORTA (MAIN ARTERY TO THE BODY)

PULMONARY ARTERY (TO THE LUNGS)

LEFT ATRIUM

PULMONARY VEIN (FROM LUNGS)

VALVE

LEFT VENTRICLE

Bloodways

Blood doesn't slosh around inside of you like lemonade inside a jug. Blood flows in a nice, neat, orderly fashion inside tubes called blood vessels.

A lot of kids, and grownups too, call all blood vessels veins. It's not so. After all, you don't call all ice cream chocolate.

There are three basic kinds of blood vessels. Each has a special job and is specially designed for its particular function along the blood highway.

Arteries handle the fast and furious rush of blood out and away from the heart. They are big muscly tubes with thick elastic walls. They are built to stand the pulsing, high-pressure blood rush. Arteries are the vessels you press when you want to count your pulse.

Capillaries (CAP ill air eze) are the tiniest blood vessels, each finer than a hair. Cap-

illaries are so tiny that blood cells must line up single file to squeeze through. The walls of these vessels are extremely thin, to allow for the in-and-out filtering of nutrients and waste products. Every cell in your body is no more than a hair's width away from a capillary.

Veins return blood to the heart and lungs. They appear as blue lines under the skin. Blood flow in the veins is a lazy river compared to the frantic rush in the arteries. The friction of the flow through the tiny capillaries slows the blood considerably. The pumping action of the heart can no longer be felt. The blood moves smoothly and slowly, so the walls of the veins are thinner. Veins have the problem of moving this slow flow without the direct pumping action of the heart. Muscle activity squeezes and pinches the veins enough to insure that the flow is not broken. Veins are also equipped with special pockets to prevent backflow.

Heart Dissection

You can get a good look at the inside parts of the heart by dissecting one. A lamb heart is a good subject because it is similar in size and shape to the human model. Meat markets tend to trim all the connecting veins and arteries away. Pick one that is as intact as you can find. Look for one that isn't split open.

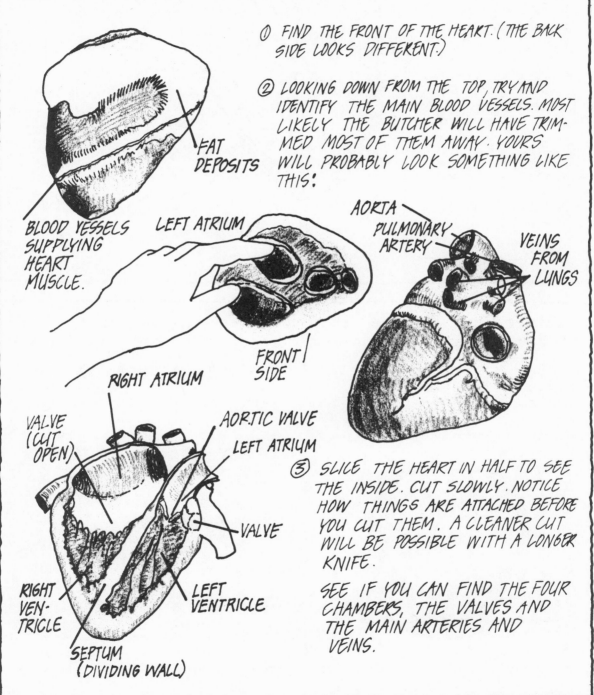

① FIND THE FRONT OF THE HEART. (THE BACK SIDE LOOKS DIFFERENT.)

② LOOKING DOWN FROM THE TOP, TRY AND IDENTIFY THE MAIN BLOOD VESSELS. MOST LIKELY THE BUTCHER WILL HAVE TRIMMED MOST OF THEM AWAY. YOURS WILL PROBABLY LOOK SOMETHING LIKE THIS:

FAT DEPOSITS

BLOOD VESSELS SUPPLYING HEART MUSCLE.

LEFT ATRIUM

AORTA

PULMONARY ARTERY

VEINS FROM LUNGS

FRONT SIDE

RIGHT ATRIUM

VALVE (CUT OPEN)

AORTIC VALVE

LEFT ATRIUM

VALVE

③ SLICE THE HEART IN HALF TO SEE THE INSIDE. CUT SLOWLY. NOTICE HOW THINGS ARE ATTACHED BEFORE YOU CUT THEM. A CLEANER CUT WILL BE POSSIBLE WITH A LONGER KNIFE.

SEE IF YOU CAN FIND THE FOUR CHAMBERS, THE VALVES AND THE MAIN ARTERIES AND VEINS.

RIGHT VENTRICLE

LEFT VENTRICLE

SEPTUM (DIVIDING WALL)

Tourniquet

Until the seventeenth century, the experts said blood was like the tide. It oozed in all directions and went no place in particular. It was then that William Harvey, an English doctor, proved that blood circulated (moved in a circle) and was pushed by the heart. Harvey showed that blood flows through the veins in only one direction — toward the heart. You can repeat the famous physician's experiment.

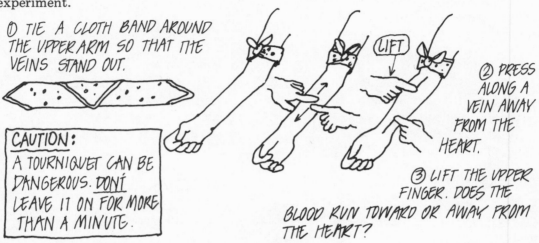

① TIE A CLOTH BAND AROUND THE UPPER ARM SO THAT THE VEINS STAND OUT.

CAUTION:
A TOURNIQUET CAN BE DANGEROUS. DON'T LEAVE IT ON FOR MORE THAN A MINUTE.

LIFT

② PRESS ALONG A VEIN AWAY FROM THE HEART.

③ LIFT THE UPPER FINGER. DOES THE BLOOD RUN TOWARD OR AWAY FROM THE HEART?

Under Your Tongue

A good place to observe living blood vessels firsthand is under your tongue. Use a mirror. A magnifying glass might also be helpful.

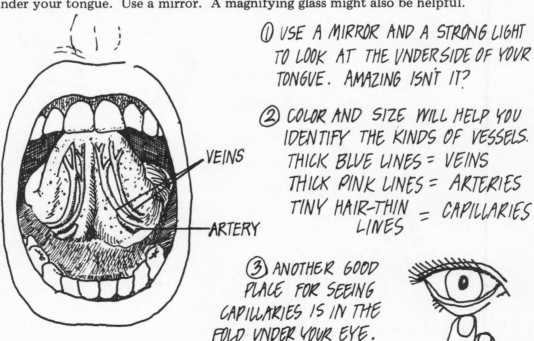

VEINS

ARTERY

① USE A MIRROR AND A STRONG LIGHT TO LOOK AT THE UNDERSIDE OF YOUR TONGUE. AMAZING ISN'T IT?

② COLOR AND SIZE WILL HELP YOU IDENTIFY THE KINDS OF VESSELS.
THICK BLUE LINES = VEINS
THICK PINK LINES = ARTERIES
TINY HAIR-THIN LINES = CAPILLARIES

③ ANOTHER GOOD PLACE FOR SEEING CAPILLARIES IS IN THE FOLD UNDER YOUR EYE.

Pulse

You can listen to a heartbeat, but you have to feel a pulse. The pulse is caused by blood stopping and starting as it rushes through your arteries. You can actually feel the elastic walls of the arteries stretching and relaxing as blood squirts by.

Arteries are generally positioned far below the skin for protection. If your aorta were suddenly cut, blood would spurt six feet into the air. Stopping such a high pressure flow is difficult at best.

Arteries surface at a few places on the body. Such spots are called pulse points. These are few and far between. Check the chart against your own.

Matchstick Pulse Meter Your pulse can be converted to a visual display, as the scientists say. You can easily make this pulse-watching device with a bit of clay and a matchstick.

① ROLL A BALL OF CLAY ABOUT THE SIZE OF A DIME. STICK A WOODEN MATCH INTO THE BALL.

YOU CAN ALSO USE A THUMBTACK BASE.

② PLACE IT ON YOUR WRIST. SHIFT IT AROUND UNTIL YOU FIND THE SPOT WITH THE STRONGEST BEAT.

OH SURE

③ IMPRESS YOUR FRIENDS. TELL THEM YOU HAVE MADE A DEVICE TO TEST CARDIAC BEAT FREQUENCY. ASK IF YOU CAN TRY IT OUT ON THEM.

SHREW
1,000X
(UP TO 1½ YEARS)

MOUSE
500X
(1-2 YEARS)

ELEPHANT
25X
(60 YEARS)

RABBIT
200X
(6 YEARS)

HUMAN
70X
(60 YEARS)

BEATS ARE GIVEN IN TIMES (X) PER MINUTE.

What Your Pulse Can Tell You

Every sort of animal has its own particular pulse rate, and its own lifespan. You
can see by looking at the chart that animals with slower pulse rates live longer.

If you are a math whiz, you have probably figured out that these mammals'
hearts are all good for about one billion
beats. With one exception.

Humans have a high-performance heart
that averages about 2.5 billion beats per
lifetime. Far beyond the average in the
animal kingdom. It isn't certain why
this is true. One thing is sure, though.
If you could slow down your heart rate,
you would have a good chance of spread-
ing those 2.5 billion beats over more
years.

Measure Your Beat Against the Athletes

It is interesting to note that athletes in
different sorts of sports have different
average pulse rates when at rest. Check
the chart. While you are concocting a
theory about these statistics, see how
your own chart measures up.

AVERAGE PERSON – 72	SPRINTER – 58
FENCER – 68	FOOT BALLER – 55
WEIGHT LIFTER – 65	OARSMAN – 50
VOLLEY-BALL PLAYER – 60	SWIMMER – 40
	RUNNER – 35 (2-6 MILES)

THESE FIGURES ARE FOR TRAINED
ATHLETES WITH EXCEPTIONALLY
LOW PULSE RATES.

Athletes Beat

Exercise gives the heart a workout.

Your first thought is probably to lie down quickly and not move a muscle. Well, you can pick yourself up off the floor, because the heart thrives on climbing stairs and running around the block.

The heart is a muscle, and like any other muscle it will respond to exercise by becoming stronger and larger. A big athletic heart can do the same amount of pumping work with fewer beats.

It is a proven fact that athletes live longer, on the average, than office workers. If you measure a lifetime in heartbeats, rather than in earth orbits around the sun, it's no wonder the heart is sometimes called the old ticker.

Stress Test

Cells are in constant need of oxygen and nourishment. Even while you sleep, your heart never stops pumping blood. Skate or straighten up your room, and the heart has to pump faster to supply those active body parts. Here is a way to survey how much harder your heart is working.

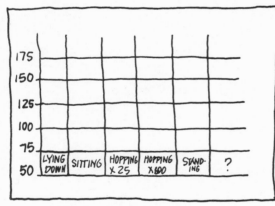

① CHECK YOUR PULSE AFTER DOING THESE ACTIVITIES. GIVE YOURSELF SOME RECOVERY TIME AFTER EACH ONE. THINK UP SOME MORE.

② CHART THE INFORMATION.

° WHAT HAPPENS TO YOUR BEAT AS YOU DO MORE WORK?
° IS SITTING OR STANDING MORE WORK?

Beat Survey

Most likely your resting pulse was higher than the supersports on the chart. Don't get excited. Kids naturally have fast pulses. As you get older your heart rate will slow. A child's beat might range from 90 to 120 beats per minute. An adult's average pulse rate is 70 beats per minute.

The best comparison is with someone your own age. If you want to know how you rate, you will need to collect your own information.

If you find you like doing surveys, you might design a survey to . . .

— test if it's true that younger people have faster beats.

— find out how body size and pulse rate are related. (Test your pets.)

— study your family and compare their rates.

Amazing Facts

— The heart circulates the body's blood more than 1,000 times per day.

— The heart pumps 5,000 to 6,000 quarts of blood per day.

— Up to 12 gallons per minute can be pumped in times of heavy exercise.

— Laid end to end, all the body's blood vessels would measure about 60,000 miles.

— Your heart is about the same size as your fist.

Lungs

AIRWAYS TO THE INSIDE

Pumpers and Separators

All animals need oxygen to live. Land
animals get oxygen from the air. Their
lungs pump in air. Their lungs also
separate out the vital oxygen so it
can be put to use inside the cells.

Lungs are both pumpers and separators.
They provide the breath of life.

Inside the Lung

Inside your chest is a tree. It is called
the *bronchial* (BRON kee al) tree. Its
job is to spread the air from the windpipe over a very wide area inside you as
quickly as possible. This is what a tree
shape does best.

We say that we breathe in air. But air
is not really inside of the body until it
passes through the lung walls into the
blood.

Warmblooded animals burn oxygen at a
furious rate. They need a lot of lung
space for moving oxygen into the blood.
That's where the tree shape comes in.

Air passing in through the windpipe di-
vides into two branches, called the bronchial tubes. These divide into little twigs
called *bronchioles* (BRON kee oles).
These twigs open into little bags called
alveoli (al VEE oh lye). Once it reaches
the alveoli, the air you breathed finally
gets under your skin, or, more accurately,
goes through the lung wall. You have
about 600 million of these spongy little
bags. That's a lot.

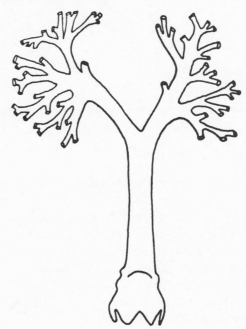

Percussing   Another way to explore your chest cavity is by *percussing* (per CUSS ing). This is the same thump test that the doctor uses. It is sort of like thumping a watermelon. If it is solid and juicy inside you get a nice, clear, ringing thump. If the melon is dried up and mealy inside, you get a fuzzy thud. You can tell a lot by thumping if you know how to listen.

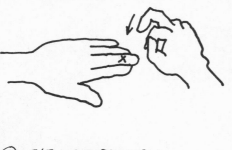

① PLACE ONE HAND FLAT ON THE BODY. STRIKE IT WITH THE THIRD FINGER OF THE OTHER HAND. PRACTICE SO YOU GET A GOOD SOUND.

② LEARN THE SOUNDS:
DULL = SOLID MUSCLE (LIKE ON THE THIGHS)
HOLLOW= AIRY PARTS (LIKE THE STOMACH)
RESONATE= AIR AND MASS (LIKE THE RIBS)

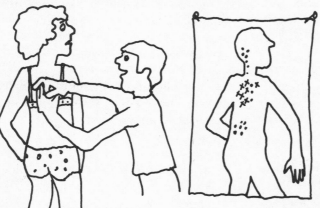

③ YOU CAN MAP THE WHOLE BODY ACCORDING TO SOUNDS TO GET A GOOD IDEA OF WHAT IS UNDERNEATH.

Locate Your Lungs

How big do you think your lungs are?

Bet you guess wrong. Most people think that they are about the size of a grapefruit, instead of the great magnificent bags they are. Actually, they're about the size of a pair of footballs and they fill the chest from neck to ribs. Here is how to go about finding yours.

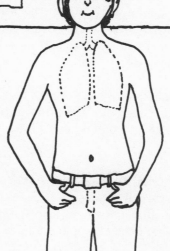

Spongy Bellows

The lungs are the pickup place for oxygen and the dumping place for carbon dioxide, the body's exhaust gas. They are continually at work breathing in air and breathing out carbon dioxide.

Inside your trunk is a room called the chest cavity. Most of the space in this room is taken up by your lungs, which hang on either side of your chest like great spongy balloons. The floor of this room is called the *diaphragm* (DIE ah fram). This muscle floor moves up and down making the room smaller and larger.

When you breathe in, the diaphragm contracts and drops down. At the same time, your ribs expand outward. The room gets larger. Air rushes in to fill the space.

When you breathe out, the diaphragm relaxes into its up position. The ribs settle down. The space shrinks and air is squeezed out of the lungs.

Contract . . . relax . . . big . . . small . . . in . . . out . . .

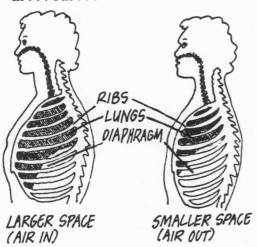

LARGER SPACE (AIR IN)   SMALLER SPACE (AIR OUT)

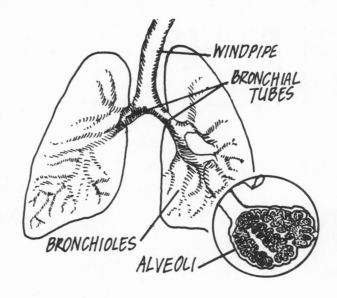

WINDPIPE
BRONCHIAL TUBES
BRONCHIOLES
ALVEOLI

Breath Rate

Sometimes your breathing is so slow and shallow that it is hardly noticeable. You often hold your breath for a moment or two when you are concentrating.

Sometimes, like after a hard-fought game of capture-the-flag, it seems you can't breathe in air fast enough.

Your rate of breathing is controlled automatically in your brain by the *respiratory* (RES purr a tory) center. Respiratory is a long word meaning having to do with breathing. The respiratory center controls your speed of breathing so that it provides just enough oxygen for every occasion, like sleeping, climbing a mountain, or squirming in your chair hoping the dentist won't call you next.

You might guess that the respiratory center makes adjustments in breath rate by measuring the blood's oxygen level. In fact, just the opposite happens. The amount of carbon dioxide wastes in the blood determine how fast you breathe.

Model Lung

You can make a working model of the lungs with a glass lamp chimney and balloon lungs. Press the diaphragm and the lungs will exhale.

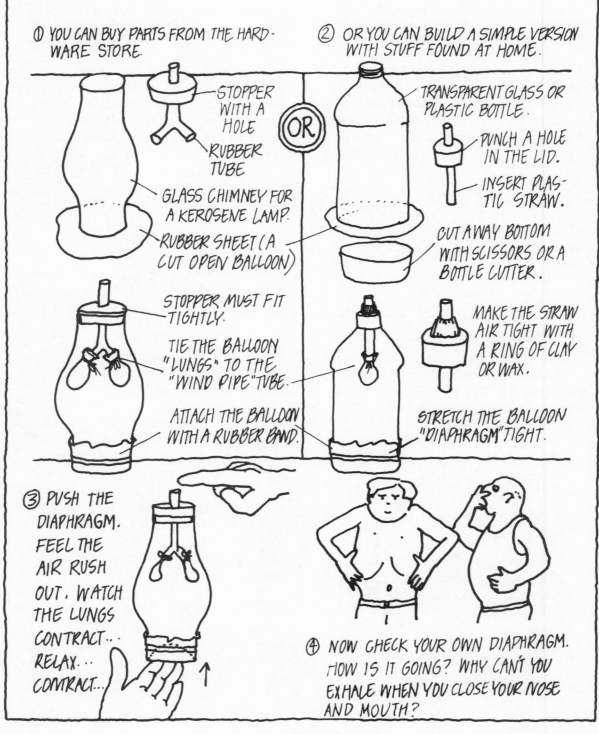

① YOU CAN BUY PARTS FROM THE HARD-WARE STORE.

STOPPER WITH A HOLE

RUBBER TUBE

OR

GLASS CHIMNEY FOR A KEROSENE LAMP.

RUBBER SHEET (A CUT OPEN BALLOON)

② OR YOU CAN BUILD A SIMPLE VERSION WITH STUFF FOUND AT HOME.

TRANSPARENT GLASS OR PLASTIC BOTTLE.

PUNCH A HOLE IN THE LID.

INSERT PLASTIC STRAW.

CUT AWAY BOTTOM WITH SCISSORS OR A BOTTLE CUTTER.

STOPPER MUST FIT TIGHTLY.

TIE THE BALLOON "LUNGS" TO THE "WIND PIPE" TUBE.

ATTACH THE BALLOON WITH A RUBBER BAND.

MAKE THE STRAW AIR TIGHT WITH A RING OF CLAY OR WAX.

STRETCH THE BALLOON "DIAPHRAGM" TIGHT.

③ PUSH THE DIAPHRAGM. FEEL THE AIR RUSH OUT. WATCH THE LUNGS CONTRACT... RELAX... CONTRACT...

④ NOW CHECK YOUR OWN DIAPHRAGM. HOW IS IT GOING? WHY CAN'T YOU EXHALE WHEN YOU CLOSE YOUR NOSE AND MOUTH?

62

Control

If you want to, you can speed up or slow down your in-out breathing cycle. This is called "voluntary control" in physiologist talk.

Most of your muscles are voluntary, including the diaphragm in your chest cavity. You can will them into action. This is handy for crossing streets behind buses, or swimming underwater.

There is also "involuntary control," which means that your nervous system is boss. For most people, no amount of wishing can slow down their heartbeat or shut off their sweat glands. Your breathing is under both voluntary and involuntary control.

If for some reason you decided to pant for a while and overdose yourself with oxygen, your involuntary control would soon take over. You would faint, and your breathing would slow until normal oxygen levels in you were restored.

On the other hand, if you decided on oxygen starvation as a way to teach your mean old stepsisters a lesson, you would be in for a surprise. Involuntary control would put you on faint and restore breathing. So you can't hold your breath until you die — no matter how hard you try.

Charting Oxygen Intake Running a 100-yard dash requires about seven quarts of oxygen. There is one quart available in your blood. Fast breathing supplies the rest. How fast your cells are working can be measured by how fast they are using oxygen. Try testing yours at various times of the day and after different sorts of activities. Measure your oxygen uptake in breaths per minute. Compare your rates with someone your size.

o YOU NEED A CLOCK WITH A SECOND HAND.

o CHECK YOUR BREATH PATTERNS ALL DAY LONG. COMPARE YOUR RATE WHEN YOU GET ANGRY WITH YOUR FIRST-THING-IN-THE-MORNING RATE. HOW DO YOU BREATHE WHEN YOU CONCENTRATE?

o FIND OUT IF THERE IS A RELATION TO WEIGHT-SIZE AND RATE. CHART YOUR ANIMAL FRIENDS.

ACTIVITY	TIME	RATE
AT REST	8AM	60

Lung Capacity

Lung Capacity You can measure your lung capacity with a spirometer. Here's how to make one with stuff from around the house.

① YOU WILL NEED A GALLON JAR, A FUNNEL, A RUBBER HOSE, AND A SINK TO SET THE DEVICE IN.

WRITE ON A PIECE OF TAPE

360 300 240 180 120 60

USE A FUNNEL OR CUT-AWAY PLASTIC BOTTLE:

SLITS FOR HOSE

X

¼ CUP = 60 MILLILITERS

WATER LEVEL MUST COVER MEETING PLACE

② STARTING FROM THE BOTTOM, MEASURE OFF THE JAR. POUR FROM A MEASURING CUP TO GET 60 MILLILITER MARKS.

③ SET UP THE SPIROMETER. FILL THE JUG WITH WATER. HOLD YOUR THUMB OVER THE MOUTH AND FLIP THE JUG. DON'T REMOVE YOUR THUMB UNTIL THE BOTTLE IS UNDER WATER SO THE BOTTLE WILL STAY FULL.

④ TEST A NORMAL SIZE BREATH BY EXHALING INTO THE HOSE. THEN AN EXTRA LARGE BREATH.
○ WHAT IS YOUR CAPACITY?

Amazing Facts

— Lungs are the only organ in the body light enough to float on water.

— The total surface area of the lungs is about 25 times that of the body's skin surface.

— The lungs secrete a detergent substance. This greatly reduces the surface tension of the fluid lining, allowing air in.

In the Bag

In the Bag   A good way to prove that something is happening to the air you breathe is to try breathing it several times. If it becomes unbreathable, then you can be certain some changes are happening within your lungs.

CAUTION: BREATH IS A MATTER OF LIFE AND DEATH. TRY THIS EXPERIMENT ONCE. THEN DISCARD THE PLASTIC BAG.

① USE A SMALL FLAT PLASTIC BAG.

② BREATHE INTO THE BAG ONCE. FORM A SNUG SEAL OVER YOUR NOSE AND MOUTH WITH YOUR FINGERS.

③ HOW MANY TIMES CAN YOU INHALE THE SAME BREATH BEFORE IT GETS UNCOMFORTABLE? STOP WHEN IT DOES!

④ KNOT THE BAG SO THAT THE EXHALED GAS CAN'T ESCAPE.

○ WHAT HAPPENED TO YOUR RESPIRATION RATE?

○ WHY DID IT CHANGE?

○ WHAT IS THE LIQUID IN THE BAG?

Lung Exhaust

Lung Exhaust   What goes in doesn't necessarily come out. You may breathe in icy, dry, foggy, hot, or dusty air. But when you breathe it out, it's warm and moist every time. There are changes happening to the air you breathe, changes you can't see or feel. You can test your lung exhaust by comparing it to a bag of air of the same size.

BURNING FOOD IS A LOT LIKE A CANDLE BURNING. HOW DOES LUNG EXHAUST AFFECT IT?

① CAREFULLY POUR A BAG OF AIR OVER A BURNING CANDLE THAT HAS BEEN SET IN A GLASS.

② POUR A BAG OF LUNG EXHAUST OVER THE CANDLE ..... WELL?

Air Conditioner in Your Nose

The nose is connected to some inner tunnels called nasal passages. These tunnels connect your nose with your windpipe. Besides being the air highway to the lungs, the nasal passages have another job. They act as an air conditioner, warming and moistening the air so that it doesn't damage the delicate lung tissue.

These airways are lined with a sticky damp material called *mucus* (MEW cus). Some people look down on mucus (also known as snot) as being one of those things they would rather not discuss. Mucus, like all body parts, does a necessary job. Mucus helps moisten the passing air. It also filters and traps foreign particles like sawdust or smoke.

Tiny hairs called *cilia* (SILLY a) line the passages to help strain out gunk. The passages themselves are built in a curvy way that forces the air to flow topsy-turvy, changing direction many times. This gives it a good chance to be warmed, wetted, and strained.

Plain As the Nose on Your Face

The nose is the only thing that sticks out on the human face.

Have you ever asked yourself, "Just why does my nose stick out?"

No?

Someone has, because there is a theory about the human nose. This theory says humans from various parts of the earth have noses that have adapted to best breathe the air of their native region.

People from hot, dry climates have long noses to make the length of moisturizing passageways as long as possible.

People from warm, steamy places, like Africa and southern India, have no need for a lot of damp nasalways. Their noses are short and flat.

People from the cold, northern climates have long narrow noses for warming and wetting cold, dry air.

PEOPLE FROM HOT, DRY CLIMATES HAVE LONG NOSES INCREASING THE LENGTH OF MOISTURIZING.

PEOPLE FROM WARM, STEAMY CLIMATES HAVE SHORTER NOSES.

PEOPLE FROM COLD CLIMATES HAVE LONG NOSES TO WARM AIR.

Nose and Throat Connection

The insides of your nose, mouth, throat, and ear passages are all interconnected. This is something you forget. You can demonstrate it with air games. Just follow the breath of air:

① BREATHE IN AND OUT OF YOUR NOSE WITH BOTH OR EITHER NOSTRIL.

② BREATHE IN AND OUT OF YOUR MOUTH.

③ BREATHE IN YOUR NOSE AND OUT OF YOUR MOUTH AND VICE VERSA.

④ SWALLOW A MOUTHFUL OF AIR IN REVERSE. CAN YOU BURP UP A MOUTHFUL?

⑤ HOLD YOUR NOSE AND SWALLOW TO CLOSE DOWN YOUR EAR PASSAGES. TO REVERSE, YAWN.

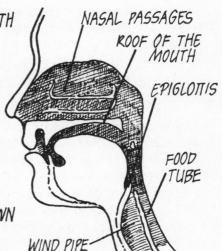

NASAL PASSAGES
ROOF OF THE MOUTH
EPIGLOTTIS
FOOD TUBE
WIND PIPE

Coughs

The *epiglottis* (epee GLOT is) is a flap that covers the windpipe. Sometimes it makes a mistake and allows a bit of food to pass down your windpipe. This tends to happen at dinner when you are trying to talk and swallow at the same time. Too big a mistake by your epiglottis could block your windpipe severely enough to be fatal. So there is some wisdom to the line, don't talk with your mouth full.

Luckily, Mother Nature knew people would always talk at the table. Thus, the cough was invented to prevent you from choking on your words.

Contact around the epiglottis sets off an explosive blast of air designed to blow any intruder clear of the area. Some-times these winds reach speeds of up to seventy miles per hour. The intruder doesn't have to be very large to set off the cough control. Mucus from a cold, dripping along the back of your throat, will set it off. You can cough yourself into exhaustion until the cold goes away.

Hiccups

Every once in a while, for some unknown reason, your diaphragm goes into spasms of contractions. As it contracts, air rushes into your lungs. To stop this rush, the epiglottis claps down over the windpipe. This stops the flow so quickly that the whole body suffers a jolt.

Hic is the sound of air rushing in. Cup is the clap-down of the epiglottis.

Throat Strings

A string pulled tight and set into motion makes a sound. This happens when the wind whistles through telephone wires, and it happens in your throat.

Your *larynx* (LAIR inks), or voice box, is a set of strings that vibrates as the inner winds blow past it.

Your larynx is located at the top of your windpipe, or trachea, at the spot known as the Adam's apple.

The strings inside the larynx are called vocal cords. Vocal cords are bands of tissue called cartilage, stretched across the windpipe. When you hum, you are passing air through your vocal cords and making them vibrate. The faster the air, the faster and louder the vibrations. Tensing your cords (stretching them to a tight and thin position) makes high-pitched, squeaky sounds. Relaxing them (to a loose and wide position) makes low, deep sounds.

Men generally have deeper voices because their cords are usually thicker and longer (about one inch). Smaller people like women and kids have cords about half an inch long. Shorter cords produce higher voices.

However talented your vocal cords may be, they couldn't be heard unless you had some sort of amplifying equipment. The chest cavity, mouth, and nasal passages all act as a resonating chamber. Shouting into a cave produces a resonating effect. Your voice bounces out big and booming.

The same way, when you talk, the sounds bounce around inside your nose, mouth, and chest, and are amplified. This echo system gives your voice its own special overtones. Because no two people have exactly the same shape of nose, mouth, or chest, no two voices are exactly alike.

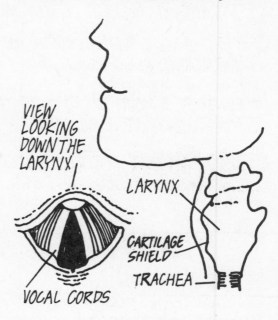

Locate Your Larynx

You can find your larynx just behind the bump in your throat called the Adam's apple. Yes, everybody has an Adam's apple. It just sticks out more on people with skinny necks. Feel around for the cartilage shield. The larynx lies directly behind.

Make the lowest noise you can. Feel the vibes?

Now make the highest sound you can.

Go up and down the scale a couple of times. Can you feel the muscles adjusting the tension for the changes in pitch?

Speech — Lip Juggling

Human animals have well-developed voice boxes. But then so do chimpanzees.

Humans have mouths, lips, teeth, and tongues, which give them the ability to form words. But then so do chimpanzees.

What humans have that chimpanzees don't is a well-developed brain that can coordinate the complicated task of word making.

Speech is made by many tiny motions of the lips, teeth, tongue, and jaws, with some help from the nasal passages. These motions happen in a rapid-fire, continuous stream and require tremendous teamwork on the part of your mind and muscles.

When you were very young, you spent thousands of hours learning how to talk. Now juggling your lips and tongue to produce the sound code is something you do almost effortlessly.

Sinus

Within the bones of your face are eight hollow spaces that are known as sinus cavities. If you watch TV, you are no doubt acquainted with the miracles that drug companies have worked on sinus agony.

A sinus is part of your nasal air conditioning system. It helps keep your nasal passageways moist by producing mucus.

Sinuses were designed to drain by gravity. This happened before humans took to

---

Hold Your Tongue
The only time you ever notice your tongue is when it happens to get caught in your biting machinery. Usually it manages to stay out of the way and still perform all the fine movements needed to make words. Do these exercises to find out what a fine job your tongue does.

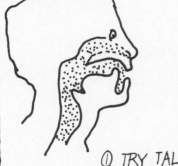 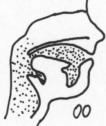

① TRY TALKING WHILE YOU HOLD YOUR TONGUE. WHEN DOES IT LIFT? WIDEN? THICKEN? CURL? TOUCH YOUR TEETH?

② TALK, BUT DON'T MOVE YOUR LIPS.
③ TALK, BUT DON'T MOVE YOUR JAWS.
④ TALK, HOLDING A MARBLE UNDER YOUR TONGUE. DON'T SWALLOW IT!

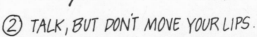

walking on two feet. In our upright posture drainage isn't very efficient. When overproduction occurs, like during a cold, the sinus cavities tend to block up. This causes a stuffy feeling or sometimes a headache.

What the drug companies don't tell you is that relief might lie in five minutes on all fours.

Special Events

Cold in your nose. Certain viruses find nasal passages the ideal home. When they move in and begin to multiply, your body answers with all its defenses. This can be pretty hard on your head. Your mucus production is stepped up to help flush out the villains. This is the familiar runny nose. The blood vessels in your nasal passages swell, giving you an angry, red nose. Meanwhile you are having trouble breathing because all that fluid has blocked your nose. To top it off, the draining mucus is tickling your sneeze reflex, and you are exploding like crazy. Horrible, isn't it?

Hayfever. Sometimes all of the cold-in-your-nose symptoms are set loose by tiny pollen particles in the air. Some people's noses treat these particles like any other harmless bits of foreign matter. They are filtered out and done away with. But some people's systems are so protective that they treat these pollens as a real threat. They launch a full-scale defense, with all the same reactions they would use for a virus attack. The result is the same miserable state of swollen-up nose and runny eyes. Luckily, pollens hang about mostly in the air in the spring and fall. Hayfever victims are safe in the winter and summer — unless they catch cold.

Yawns. Enforced quiet, like sitting in a chair while your teacher talks about fractions, may lead to shallow breathing. Shallow breathing seems to trigger falling asleep. To keep from falling asleep, you take in a gasp of air, or yawn, to break the shallow breathing cycle. Then you try to hide your yawning mouth with your hand. Unfortunately, your fractions teacher knows yawning is dangerously close to falling asleep.

Cells

BASIC BODY BITS

There is a name for the stuff from which all living matter is made. It is called *protoplasm* (PRO toe plazum), which means "first stuff." Protoplasm is a clear jelly-like substance made out of ordinary everyday chemicals like carbon, nitrogen, hydrogen, and oxygen. However, this jelly is different from your everyday chemicals. It can eat, breathe, and excrete. This jelly is alive!

All living things are made out of the same basic protoplasm organized into neat little packages called cells. Cells are the basic units of life. They come in different sizes and shapes. However, whale cells and mouse cells are about the same size. It's the vast difference in cell numbers and organization that accounts for the surprising variety of sizes and shapes of living things.

Cell City

All living things are made out of cells. Some creatures are microscopic, jellylike things having only one cell, while some animals are monstrous hunks of lumbering protoplasm made up of billions or even trillions of cells. In both kinds of animals, each cell is equally alive and equally eager to carry on the basic work of staying alive.

But the work of a cell in a many-celled body is different because of something called specialization. The cells work together in teams, each team performing only one of the many jobs necessary to stay alive. For instance, a cell might take on the job of moving oxygen around the body, in the blood. While it is at work, other cells are busy taking care of the fuel supply, communications, and waste removal.

Specialization happens outside of bodies as well as inside them. A person who lives in a city doesn't keep cows, bake his own bread, make his own shoes, or run his own hospital. He specializes in something like fixing TVs and leaves the other services to somebody else.

Even though you think of yourself as a whole body, you are also a colony of about 100 trillion smaller parts, your cells. All these parts are working in a vast and complicated unison. You are a cell city.

100 TRILLION HAMBURG-ERS WOULD MAKE A WALL 13' HIGH, 1' WIDE, LONG ENOUGH TO CIRCLE THE EARTH.

Problems You Didn't Know You Had

Trees, horned toads, banana slugs, and people all have problems. Amazingly, they have many of the same problems. Right off the bat you probably think you don't have a thing in common with a banana slug.

Okay, you're partly right. Horned toads don't lose library books, and banana slugs don't lose their best friends when their family moves to Sioux City. But these critters do share with you some very basic problems. You could call them basic survival problems, or, if you like, the big five problems of staying alive:

1. Living things must eat.

2. Living things must breathe.

3. Living things must get rid of wastes.

4. Living things must be sensitive to their environments, moving toward things like light and food, and away from things which could be harmful, like poison ivy or broken glass.

5. Living things must reproduce.

Actually, you have a few things in common with banana slugs besides problems. You are both made up of protoplasm organized into cell cities. But although you share the same problems of staying alive, your ways of solving them are as different as wasps and wooly mammoths.

You Always Have a Temperature

The nurse pokes a thermometer into your mouth and says, "Well, dearie, let's see if you have a temperature." What this really means is, "Let's see if your temperature is different from normal." (Even ice cubes have a temperature.)

All your cells are constantly taking in chemical fuel and burning it to produce energy for you. This process also produces much heat. That's why you are warmer than this book just now.

Another word for these chemical reactions happening inside your cells is *metabolism* (me TAB o liz um). Sometimes, like when you are running to catch the bus, your cells are going full blast. Other times, like when you are sleeping, your cells have slowed down to idle speed.

The speed at which your cells are burning fuel is called your metabolic rate. Your body can adjust to a wide variety of metabolic rates. Dashing for the bus can rev up your rate to almost forty times what it is when you are asleep.

So when you get poked with a thermometer, don't be fooled. A nurse already knows you have a temperature, and is just getting an idea of how things are going inside your cells.

Cell Fires

Each one of your hundred trillion cells needs fuel to perform its special job.

Each one of your cells has the ability to take in chemicals and combine them with oxygen to make energy.

This process is called *oxidation* (ox i DAY shun). Oxidation is not a rare event. It happens all around you every day. Sometimes it happens slowly, as when iron combines with oxygen to form rust. When you bite into an apple and it sits for a while and turns brown, that too is oxidation. When oxidation happens rapidly, it is called burning.

Climate Control Chart

Some people like nothing better than baking in a sauna, then rolling in the snow. Our systems can take a shocking variation in temperature as long as it's on the outside. However, our internal climates must be maintained as carefully as any hothouse full of rare orchids.

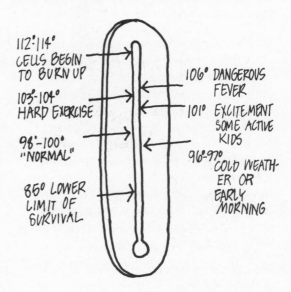

112°-114° CELLS BEGIN TO BURN UP

103°-104° HARD EXERCISE

98°-100° "NORMAL"

85° LOWER LIMIT OF SURVIVAL

106° DANGEROUS FEVER

101° EXCITEMENT SOME ACTIVE KIDS

96°-97° COLD WEATHER OR EARLY MORNING

Taking a Temperature

The normal human temperature is 98.6 degrees Fahrenheit. Normal for you may be a degree or so above or below "normal." It is good to know what is normal for you. Probably there is a thermometer in the family medicine chest; or you can buy one at any drug store.

① SHAKE THE THERMOMETER— SO THAT IT READS 96° OR LESS. CLEAN IT WITH SOAPY WATER OR ALCOHOL. RINSE.

② PUT THE BULB UNDER YOUR TONGUE FOR 3 MINUTES. DON'T TRY TO TALK.

③ READ IT.

④ WASH IT.

TRY TAKING YOUR TEMPERATURE AT DIFFERENT TIMES, LIKE IN THE MORNING, AFTER A COLD SHOWER, OR A FIVE-MILE HIKE.

Hot Blood

A frog in a 70 degree pond is a 70 degree frog. A frog in a 40 degree pond is a 40 degree frog, and is moving very slowly, if at all.

A kid in a 70 degree pond is a 98 degree kid. A kid in a 40 degree pond is still a 98 degree kid, although you can bet he's swimming as fast as he can to get out.

One difference between kids and frogs is the difference between warmblooded and coldblooded beings. People have automatic climate control inside their bodies. Their bodies keep themselves at an even temperature by carefully controlling the rate of burning in their cells. Coldblooded creatures have no internal temperature control. Their rate of metabolism is determined by their environment. When the outside temperature drops way down, all their body processes slow way down.

Humans, and all mammals, are souped-up hot-blooded beings. Their metabolisms are speedy, but are kept at an even keel.

So no matter what the temperature is outside, the climate on the inside is ever warm and ready for action.

Special Events

Fever is when your body's temperature control is set above normal. Fever is a sign that your body is fighting off an infection. It is thought that fever does two things. When the temperature rises, the body's chemical actions speed up so that damaged tissues can be repaired more quickly. Also, virus or bacteria invaders don't survive well at high temperatures. Perhaps fever is the body's attempt to cook them into submission.

Chills. You have a high temperature and cold skin. You are hot inside, but still you shiver. Chills are your body's way of creating a fever. The muscle action from shivering produces heat, which raises your temperature in an effort to fight off infection. When the crisis is over, your temperature is set back to normal, the skin warms, and you sweat.

Burn a Burger

The kind of rapid-fire burning that happens to a board has a lot in common with the slower, more controlled burning that happens within your cells.

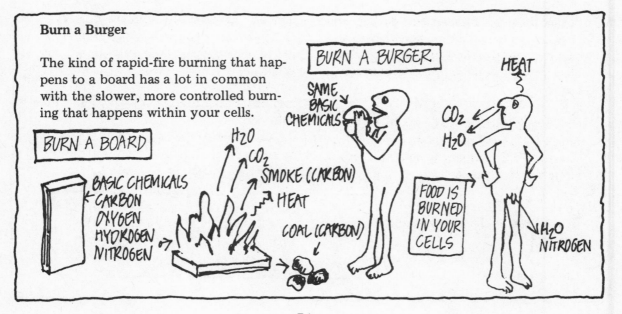

Digestion

DOWN THE FOOD TUBE

Once you swallow food, can you safely say it is inside your body? Not really.

It is inside the food tube, which is a thirty-foot-long, winding canal that leads from your mouth to your anus. Strictly speaking, food is not inside the body until it is absorbed through the walls of this tube.

Before those big hunks of candy bars and chunks of peanut butter sandwiches can pass through the food tube walls, they must be broken down into simpler substances.

This breakdown doesn't happen all at once. It's a long process with many phases. These happen at many places along the food canal.

Which Bunch Are You for Lunch?

All living things need fuel to carry on their life's work.

On earth there are two basic ways of getting fuel — two basic ways of making a living.

One way is to create your own food internally using sunlight. Only certain creatures are equipped to do this. They are called plants.

The other is to eat living (or formerly living) things. This is how the animal kingdom survives. Since all living things are made of pretty much the same stuff, any creature can serve on the menu of any other creature. If not directly, then indirectly.

In the animal kingdom, getting something into your mouth is only half the battle. The other half is breaking up the chemicals of the swallowed thing into something your body can use.

This process is called *digestion* (die JEST shun) — and it's amazing.

Breakdown

Your teeth and tongue take the first steps in battering food into bits. As they are shredding and grinding, *saliva* (sah LIVE ah) is squirted into the food to moisten and soften it. Saliva contains a chemical called an *enzyme* (EN zime), which breaks down starches in the food.

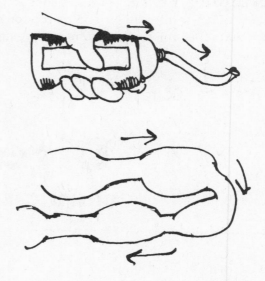

When you are done chewing, you swallow, and the mouthful of pulpy bits makes its way down the food canal or, *esophagus* (e SOF ah gus), to the stomach. Food does not free-fall into the stomach like a stone dropping into a well. The food is squeezed along by muscles in the esophagus. You could swallow standing on your head.

In the stomach, food is treated to a strong acid bath, as it is churned about by the stomach's muscular walls. These walls are protected by a mucus lining, which saves the stomach from its own acidic juice. Any break in the lining, and in a couple of hours the stomach will have eaten a hole in itself.

The exit from the stomach opens up every few minutes and squirts a couple of spoonfuls of food into the small intestine. By now the food has become a mashed-up milky liquid.

The *small intestine* (in TEST in) is a long, curly tube with a shaggy lining. It is equipped with its own set of digestive juices for final food breakdown. The walls of this tube hug and push the food along in an action called *peristalsis* (perry STAL sis).

Peristalsis puts the squeeze on food muscles in the intestinal wall. They contract and relax, forcing the food around and through. It's the same way you might squeeze a tube of toothpaste. All this squishing and squeezing makes a lot of noise. Put your ear to a friend's intestine and you'll hear all sorts of sloshes, squirts, and rumbles. The next time somebody gives you the evil eye because your guts rumble, remember a healthy belly is never silent.

The walls of the small intestine are lined with millions of tiny fingerlike things called *villi* (VILL eye) that stick out into the passing chemical soup. They absorb the valuable parts of the broken-down food into the bloodstream. At last you can say that the food is in the body.

Non-useful parts of the food continue to move along to the solid waste section called the large intestine. Although it is still a mover, not much happens in the large intestine except the absorption of water. As water is absorbed, the waste gets thicker and thicker. Finally it piles up in a fairly thick mass, waiting to be ejected through the anus.

Keeping Track Ask someone to point to their stomach, and they will often show off their intestines — and their poor knowledge of anatomy. Locate your stomach and some other points of interest along your digestive tract.

STOMACH IS BETWEEN THE RIBS ABOVE THE WAIST.

ESOPHAGUS CAN SOMETIMES BE FELT WHEN YOU TAKE A SWALLOW OF COLD WATER.

LARGE INTESTINE LIES JUST BELOW THE WAIST.

SMALL INTESTINE SITS UNDER YOUR BELLY BUTTON. LISTEN IN AFTER LUNCH.

Charting the Food Tube

Breaking food down is a long process. It happens at various stages along the food tube. Check the chart to find out what happens where.

LIVER, PANCREAS AND GALLBLADDER. - ALL MAKE CHEMICALS FOR FOOD BREAKDOWN

SMALL INTESTINE - FINAL DIGESTION AND ABSORPTION. THIS TRIP TAKES 8 HOURS THROUGH A SHAGGY TUBE 20 FEET LONG.

VILLI

LARGE INTESTINE - COLLECTS THE DISCARDS LIKE PLANT FIBERS (CELERY STRINGS), SEEDS, OLD BLOOD CELLS. ALSO RECYCLES WATER.

MOUTH - ENTRANCE TO THE FOOD TUBE. SHREDDING AND STARCH BREAKDOWN.

ESOPHAGUS - MUSCULAR TUBE THAT CAN SQUEEZE FOOD TO THE STOMACH IN 7 SECONDS.

STOMACH, ACID BATH. CHURNING BREAKS DOWN PROTEIN. FOOD STAYS HERE 3-4 HOURS. IT HOLDS UP TO 1½ QUARTS.

PANCREAS

ANUS - WASTE EXIT FROM THE FOOD TUBE

ESOPHAGUS

LIVER

GALLBLADDER

STOMACH

LARGE INTESTINE

SMALL INTESTINE

APPENDIX

Amazing Enzyme

There are about seven hundred different enzymes in the body. *Amylase* (AM ah layse), the starch-into-sugar enzyme of the mouth, is one of many. Their jobs include food breakdown and controlling the release of energy in the body. For instance, a slice of chocolate cake contains enough energy to raise the temperature of a 100-pound person to 117 degrees Fahrenheit. That is enough heat to fry your brains. Enzyme control is very important.

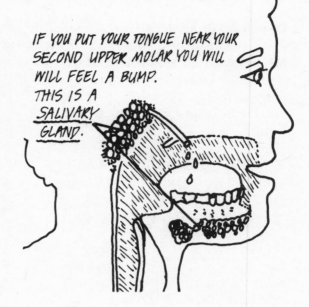

IF YOU PUT YOUR TONGUE NEAR YOUR SECOND UPPER MOLAR YOU WILL WILL FEEL A BUMP. THIS IS A _SALIVARY GLAND._

Starch and Spit Test

You can taste the work of the enzyme that breaks down starch into sugar. All you need is a soda cracker and a couple of minutes.

① CHEW A SODA CRACKER WELL. HOLD IT IN YOUR MOUTH FOR FIVE MINUTES.

② WHAT DOES YOUR MOUTH TELL YOU ABOUT THE ACTION OF AMYLASE?

YOU CAN SEE ENZYME ACTION WITH THIS TEST:

I TABLESPOON CORN STARCH

STIR INTO I CUP BOILING WATER

I TABLESPOON SALIVA

2 TABLESPOONS STARCH SOLUTION

USE THE TEST FOR STARCH ON THE NEXT PAGE.

① MAKE UP THE STARCH SOLUTION. LET IT COOL.

② MIX THE STARCH AND SALIVA. EVERY MINUTE REMOVE A TEASPOONFUL TO A CLEAN DISH.

③ TEST IT FOR STARCH. WHAT IS HAPPENING?

Chemical Lunch

Maybe you think that you would be a lot happier eating only dessert. But your body wouldn't. It's tuned to run on a number of basic sorts of foods.

These fall into three groups, which are different according to their chemical makeup. Each of these food types performs a specific job, although they are somewhat interchangeable.

— *Carbohydrates* (car bow HI drates) are fuel foods. These are the starch and sugar foods like cornflakes, donuts, bread, spaghetti, or potatoes.

— Proteins are building blocks for body repair and growth. These tend to be in meaty sorts of foods, usually from animal sources like chicken, eggs, steak, cheese, or hot dogs, or in beans and grain foods.

—Fats are for energy production. They are the oily foods like butter, cream, or margarine.

Often foods fall into a combination of these groups, like peanut butter, which is both fat and protein. Or ice cream, which contains fat, carbohydrate, and protein.

Kitchen Chemistry
Find the group, or groups, to which your favorite foods belong. You can perform chemical tests in your kitchen at home.

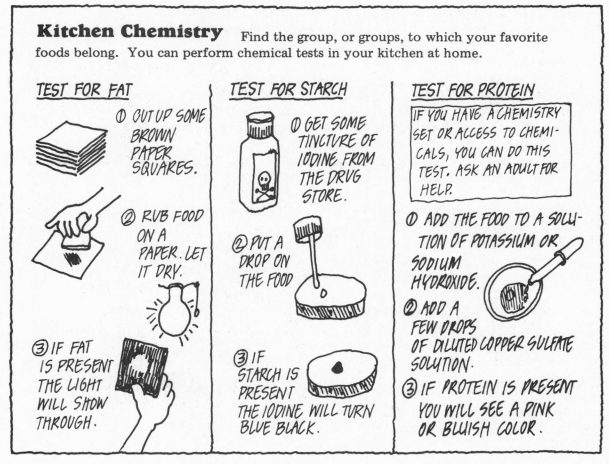

TEST FOR FAT

① CUT UP SOME BROWN PAPER SQUARES.

② RUB FOOD ON A PAPER. LET IT DRY.

③ IF FAT IS PRESENT THE LIGHT WILL SHOW THROUGH.

TEST FOR STARCH

① GET SOME TINCTURE OF IODINE FROM THE DRUG STORE.

② PUT A DROP ON THE FOOD

③ IF STARCH IS PRESENT THE IODINE WILL TURN BLUE BLACK.

TEST FOR PROTEIN

IF YOU HAVE A CHEMISTRY SET OR ACCESS TO CHEMICALS, YOU CAN DO THIS TEST. ASK AN ADULT FOR HELP.

① ADD THE FOOD TO A SOLUTION OF POTASSIUM OR SODIUM HYDROXIDE.

② ADD A FEW DROPS OF DILUTED COPPER SULFATE SOLUTION.

③ IF PROTEIN IS PRESENT YOU WILL SEE A PINK OR BLUISH COLOR.

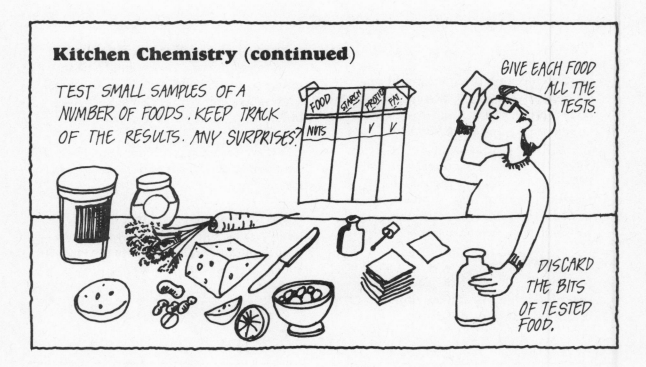

Kitchen Chemistry (continued)

TEST SMALL SAMPLES OF A NUMBER OF FOODS. KEEP TRACK OF THE RESULTS. ANY SURPRISES?

FOOD	STARCH	PROTEIN	FAT
NUTS		✓	✓

GIVE EACH FOOD ALL THE TESTS.

DISCARD THE BITS OF TESTED FOOD.

Riddle of the Sphincter

At the end of the intestines is an opening called the *anus* (AY nus). (It has other names in less polite circles.) Around the anus is a ring of muscles called a *sphincter* (SFINK ter). This sphincter is able to open up by relaxing and to close down by contracting. It works sort of like the cord around the hood of a raincoat.

You have other sphincters. There is one in your eye that opens and closes to let more or less light in. You also have one around your lips, which could be thought of as your kissing muscle.

When your lower intestine gets full, nerve sensors send a message to your brain. At a convenient time you can voluntarily re-lax your anal sphincter and empty your large intestine.

The riddle is: Why do people get squirmy when you mention sphincters?

Solid Waste

Not everything you put in your mouth can be broken down by your digestive juices. What can't be digested makes the trip down the food canal and is pushed out through the far end as solid waste.

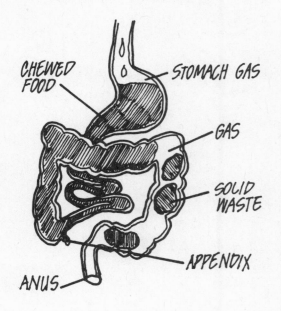

CHEWED FOOD

STOMACH GAS

GAS

SOLID WASTE

APPENDIX

ANUS

The proper name for this solid waste is *feces* (FEE sees). Normal human feces are about one-fourth dead intestinal bacteria. They also contain some digestive juices and some water and indigestible material. This material might be cellulose, which is a plant fiber like the strings in celery. Or it might be all sorts of accidentally swallowed things like dirt, bubble gum, or bits of fingernails.

Bacteria for Life

Your intestines contain a whole population of *bacteria* (back TEAR e ah). Bacteria are tiny one-celled creatures, about nine hundred times too small to be seen without a microscope. It's not true that the only good bacteria are dead bacteria. Only a few are troublemakers for humans.

In fact, your resident bacteria do you some good. It seems that as they devour the remains of the food in the intestines, they also secrete some helpful vitamins, like K, B_{12}, thiamine, and riboflavin. Also they are able to digest small amounts of cellulose, providing a few calories of daily nutrition.

Not only do bacteria exist in the food tube, but all over your surface, in every fold, crease, and cavity. There are considerably more bacteria living on you than there are people living on earth. A person's bacteria population amounts to ½ percent of their total weight. Before you get alarmed, you should know that animals raised in germ-free states are small and sickly. It seems we are able to maintain a healthy state of affairs with our bacteria population.

Natural Gas

One of the byproducts of food breakdown by bacteria is methane gas. As waste food piles up in the large intestine, bacteria multiply and produce increasing amounts of gas. Some foods like beans, cabbage, and brussels sprouts are not very digestible. They leave a lot of leftovers for your bacteria to work on. They are notorious gas producers.

Cooking With Gas
(A Natural Fact)

You may be surprised to know that natural gas is just that. The methane that powers the kitchen range was produced from the breakdown of ancient plants by the very sort of bacteria you have in your intestines. A sort of underground fart from a prehistoric salad.

YOUR BODY'S BACTERIA COULD FILL A SOUP CAN. SUBTRACT THOSE WHICH LIVE IN THE GUT AND THE REST COULD ALL HIDE IN A THIMBLE.

Special Events

Hunger Pangs. Hunger contractions occur after the stomach is empty for eight to ten hours. When the stomach is not filled with food, it is filled mostly with gas. Contractions squeeze the gas against the stomach walls. You feel hunger pangs and hear growls as a result.

Vomiting. Sometimes an irritating substance gets into the gut. The body has an emergency system for removing it called throwing up. Food can be recalled all the way up to the end of the small intestine, some twenty feet down the tube. This happens by backward contractions which push the food into the stomach. Your brain is signaled that all is not well in the gut by a sensation of nausea. The trachea shuts down, the stomach relaxes. Strong contractions of the diaphragm and abdominal muscles force food up and out the food tube. You vomit.

Amazing Facts

— The average person eats 3 pounds of food each day, or 1,095 pounds of groceries a year.

— Your mouth makes about 500 milliliters (½ quart) of saliva daily. In total, your body secretes more than 7 quarts of assorted digestive juices.

— Our appendix is a remnant of a longer intestine. Grazing animals use this organ for fermentation.

Kidneys
WASHING MACHINES FOR THE BLOOD

Next to your brain, your kidneys are some of the most complicated pieces of equipment you have. In the next minute, more than one quart of blood will pass through your kidneys. It will come out with just the right wastes removed so it can continue to carry on your life's work.

Kidneys are filters. Each is a mass of more than a million tiny filter tubes. Blood is filtered into these tubes and then out again. Wastes are captured in these tubes and left behind. These wastes drain their way out of the kidney, in the form of urine, to your bladder.

Inside the Kidney

Blood rushes into the kidney from a large artery. It flows into ever smaller vessels until it reaches a ball of tiniest vessels called a *glomerulus* (glo MER you luss). The flow changes from something like a gushing river to many meandering streams.

This ball of blood vessels is enclosed in

a capsule made of two thin walls. The slowed blood has time to filter into the surrounding membrane. All but the largest particles (like blood cells) filter through the capsule into small tubes.

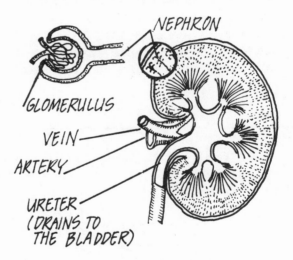

These tubes are called *nephrons* (NEFF rons), and are where the cleaning takes place. All of the valuable parts are reabsorbed into the blood. The wastes stay behind. When you dissect a lamb kidney, you will notice that all the threadlike nephrons point to the kidney's center. That is where the wastes, in the form of urine, are sent.

Urine leaves the kidneys through tubes called *ureters* (yoor RHEE ters), which lead to a storage bag called the bladder. You can sense when your bladder is full. At this point you eliminate hours of wastes in one go.

Urine

A lot of people feel a little embarrassed talking about . . . er . . . ah . . .

However, folks from other places weren't so shy when it came to putting it to use.

Many ancient peoples used it as soap. Some American Indians used it as a mouthwash. In South America it has even been sipped as a refreshing drink.

Shocking, you say? People who have found urine to be such a useful fluid would probably be surprised at the way we feel. One thing is sure. It's a matter of attitude, because urine hasn't changed any.

What Exactly Is It, Then?

This will surprise you, but healthy, fresh urine is cleaner than spit, cleaner than your hands, cleaner than the tuna sandwich you had for lunch.

Fresh urine has *no* bacteria in it. What it does contain is:

— About 95% water.

— About 5% urea (the waste from protein breakdown).

— Small amounts of normally useful substances which were filtered out of the blood because there was too much of them.

Fresh urine has a definite smell, which isn't too offensive. If it stands around it will collect bacteria, which will start its decay. The urea will eventually break down into ammonia, the same strong-smelling stuff you use to wash windows.

Liquidation   Would you like to know what your bladder capacity is? Or how much liquid passes through it each day? By keeping careful records, you can find out how long it takes your kidneys to filter those big bottles of soda pop you gulp.

A WIDE MOUTH PEANUT-BUTTER JAR WORKS WELL.

① MARK OFF THE JAR IN OUNCES. (FROM THE BOTTOM UP.)

② URINATE INTO THE JAR. RECORD THE AMOUNT. THEN RINSE THE JAR.

AMOUNT	DAY-TIME
12 oz.	6·1 -7 AM

TOTAL

∘ URINATE WHEN YOUR BLADDER IS FULL. WHAT IS YOUR MAXIMUM CAPACITY?
∘ TOTAL YOUR DAILY OUTPUT. KEEP TRACK FOR A FEW DAYS. IS THERE A PATTERN?

Find 'Em

Your kidneys hang near your spine in the middle of your back. They are protected by your bottommost ribs and are covered by layers of fat. Imagine a line across your back, drawn from elbow to elbow. Your kidneys are lurking on either side of your spine in line with your elbows.

It's no accident your kidneys are protected by ribs and fat. If anything happened to these all-important filters, it would not be many hours before you would begin to be poisoned by your own wastes.

However, humans are well-equipped in the kidney department. Should one fail, you can function quite well with the other. People have been known to survive with only one half of one healthy kidney.

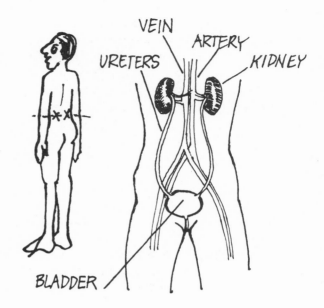

Bladder

Your bladder is a muscular bag located in the middle of your lower abdomen. It is easy to find if you haven't emptied it in a while. Give the area a poke, and your full-up feelings will let you know when you are on target.

Bladders and balloon water bombs have certain things in common. They both stretch, and they both have limits on how much they can comfortably hold. An adult bladder will hold about one quart of fluid.

A human bladder, like a water balloon, will hold liquid as long as its opening is tightly shut. A living bladder is held shut by a contracting band of muscles called a sphincter.

When these sphincter muscles around the opening become relaxed, the liquid inside rushes out, leaving a small shrunken bag.

Bladders do have certain special improvements over balloons. A bladder has three openings, or doors. It fills constantly through two of those, which are connected to tubes from the two kidneys. Your bladder also has a full-up signal system that tells you when it is time to empty. Then the bladder's strong muscular walls do a magnificent job of squeezing a full bladder down to empty.

Bladder Signals

You have special nerve endings in your bladder walls called stretch receptors. As your bladder fills, and the walls stretch, the receptors signal the brain that your internal reservoir is getting full. You take notice and think maybe you'd better take steps to do something about it.

If you are busy you might ignore the message. The signal stops and you forget about it for an hour or more. Sooner or later the signal returns. It will come faster and faster as your bladder gets fuller and fuller — until, no matter how hard you try, you can ignore it no longer. Finally, to relieve yourself of those furious messages, you urinate.

Amazing Facts

— Each day 180 quarts of blood are pumped through the kidneys. (That's 25% of the blood pumped through your heart, or as much blood as flows through 100 pounds of muscle.)

— Each kidney contains about 1 million tiny tubes, which add up to more than 40 miles in length.

Kidney Dissection

Warning: Cutting up a kidney is not for kids who are afraid of smells. Kidneys smell like blood and urine. Kids who aren't afraid of smells can ask the butcher for lambs' kidneys. They are similar in size and shape to your own.

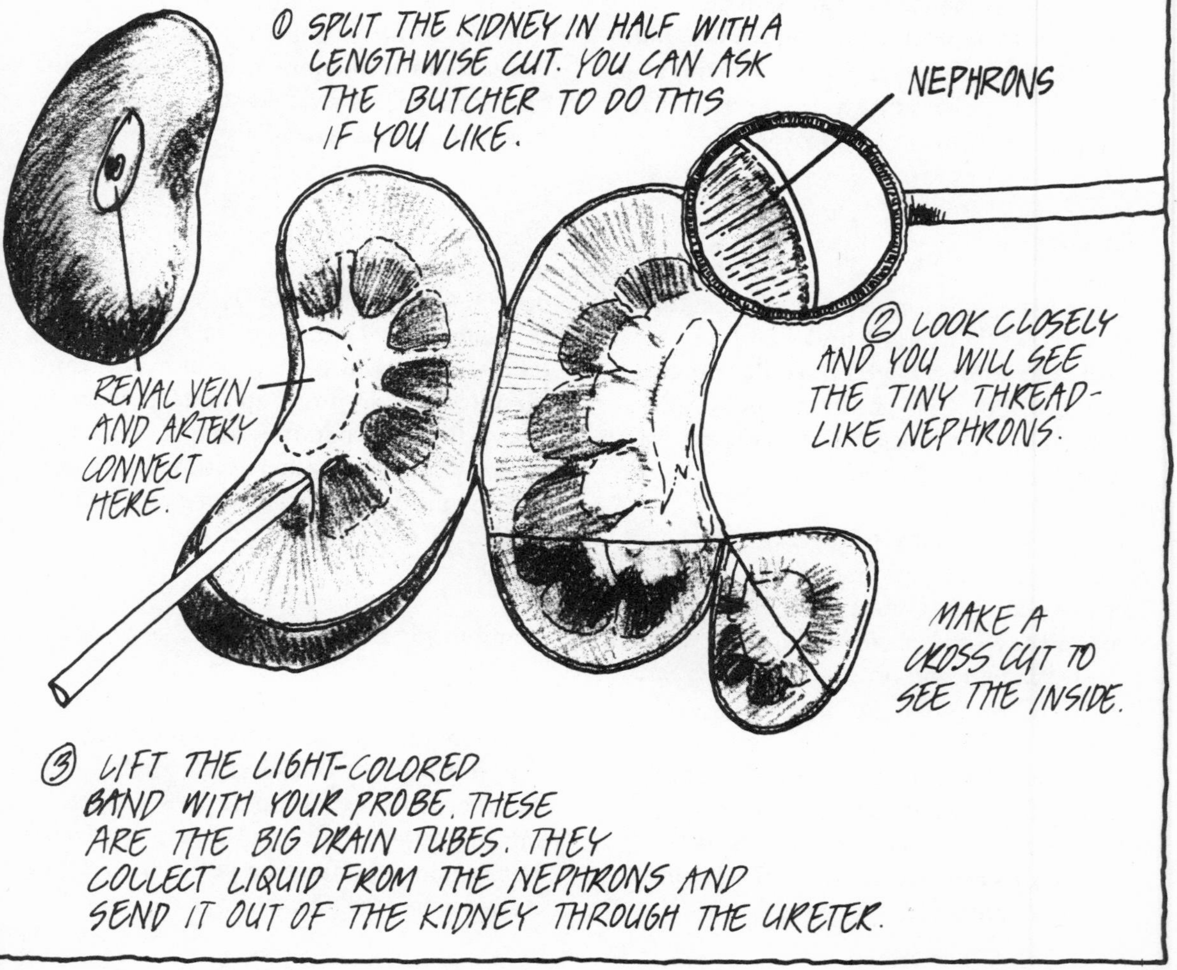

① SPLIT THE KIDNEY IN HALF WITH A LENGTHWISE CUT. YOU CAN ASK THE BUTCHER TO DO THIS IF YOU LIKE.

NEPHRONS

RENAL VEIN AND ARTERY CONNECT HERE.

② LOOK CLOSELY AND YOU WILL SEE THE TINY THREAD-LIKE NEPHRONS.

MAKE A CROSS CUT TO SEE THE INSIDE.

③ LIFT THE LIGHT-COLORED BAND WITH YOUR PROBE. THESE ARE THE BIG DRAIN TUBES. THEY COLLECT LIQUID FROM THE NEPHRONS AND SEND IT OUT OF THE KIDNEY THROUGH THE URETER.

Eyes
WINDOWS ON THE WORLD

"But I don't have eyes in the back of my head." How many times have you heard that?

How many times have you given any thought to where your eyes are located?

Have a look around the animal kingdom and notice the position of the eyes on different animal faces.

Notice anything odd about yours?

Humans and the apes have a different sort of face. Flat, with both eyes front and close together.

Having eyes around at the sides of the face gives the advantage of being able to see around to the rear.

Having two eyes up front seems a silly waste of sight. If one eye were moved around to the side, or shifted to the back, certainly a lot more could be brought into view.

But this two-eyed sight, called binocular vision, gives humans and apes a special talent, the ability to see in 3-D.

Sure, we do sacrifice a good bit of our side vision, but we more than make up for it with our ability to see the world in depth. This is the talent that lets apes swing through trees, hardly missing a branch, and allows us to catch balls and drive cars.

Depth

Your ability to see depth is your ability to judge how far away an object is in space.

When you look at something, each eye is moved into looking position by a separate set of muscles.

Each eye sees the same thing from two slightly different angles.

The brain is able to use information sent by the muscles about the position of each eye. From this information it is able to judge the distance of the object.

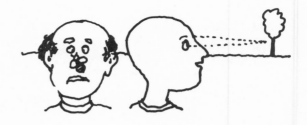

Keep Your Eye on the Ball

How well can you catch? How well can you catch using one eye? You will need a Ping-Pong ball, an eye patch, and a friend to find out. This one-eyed experience will give you some insight into just how important the teamwork of your two eyes is.

NOW I KNOW WHY THERE ARE NO ONE-EYED BIG LEAGUE BALL PLAYERS...

- YOU GET 15 TRYS TO CATCH THE BALL WITH OPEN EYES.
- THEN 15 TRYS USING ONE EYE ONLY.
- TRADE WITH YOUR PARTNER, THIS TIME YOU TOSS.
- KEEP TRACK OF YOUR SCORES. IF THIS IS TOO EASY, YOU MIGHT TRY CATCHING THE BALL WITH ONE HAND ONLY.

Seeing Is Believing

"I saw it with my own eyes" are famous words. Sometimes your eyes lie. Here is an experiment to prove it. It works on the principle that each eye sees a slightly different view of the world. For instance, you can turn two fingers into a floating hot dog.

HOLD YOUR INDEX FINGERS TIP TO TIP ABOUT 5" AWAY FROM YOUR EYES. IF YOU FOCUS ON SOME OBJECT IN THE DISTANCE, A FUZZY SAUSAGE SHAPE WILL APPEAR.

Hole in Your Hand

Two eyes are not always better than one. Sometimes two images can produce a rather muddled picture of reality. However, your brain has learned to ignore conflicting images so that you "see" an edited version of the messages your eyes send your brain. · Here is a way to look right through your hand.

① ROLL A SHEET OF PAPER INTO A TUBE.

② HOLD IT UP TO YOUR EYE LIKE A TELESCOPE.

③ HOLD YOUR OTHER HAND IN FRONT OF YOUR EYE (ABOUT 4" AWAY). IF YOU POSITION EVERY THING RIGHT, YOUR HAND WILL SEEM TO HAVE A HOLE IN IT.

Stereo Vision

Here is an experiment that will give you a good idea of what each eye sees separately, and what they see together.

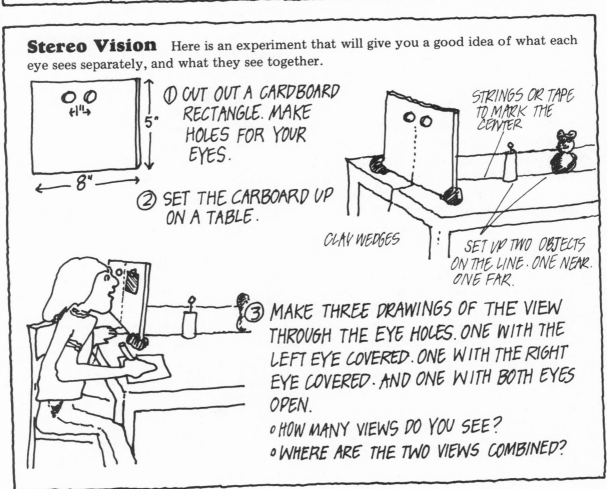

5"

8"

① CUT OUT A CARDBOARD RECTANGLE. MAKE HOLES FOR YOUR EYES.

② SET THE CARBOARD UP ON A TABLE.

CLAY WEDGES

STRINGS OR TAPE TO MARK THE CENTER

SET UP TWO OBJECTS ON THE LINE. ONE NEAR. ONE FAR.

③ MAKE THREE DRAWINGS OF THE VIEW THROUGH THE EYE HOLES. ONE WITH THE LEFT EYE COVERED. ONE WITH THE RIGHT EYE COVERED. AND ONE WITH BOTH EYES OPEN.

o HOW MANY VIEWS DO YOU SEE?

o WHERE ARE THE TWO VIEWS COMBINED?

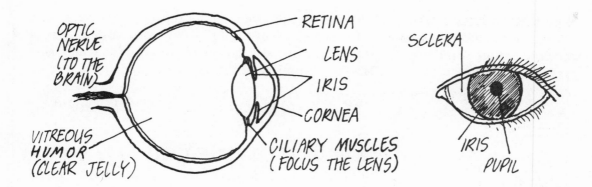

Eyes Have It

People talk about dreamy eyes, beady eyes, hawk eyes, evil eyes, misty eyes, Spanish eyes, and goo-goo eyes. Whether they know it or not, they are really talking about the face around the eyes. If you could remove some eyes and set them out on a plate, you would find that eyes look pretty much alike. With the exception of color.

Eyeball is a good name. Removed from their sockets, eyes look like balls. You can think of the eye as a tough bag, about the size of a Ping-Pong ball, filled with a clear jelly. Most of the bag is covered by a light, tight coat called the *sclera* (SKLAIR a), also known as the white of the eye.

At the front of this almost circular bag is a hole that lets in light. This hole is covered by a clear cover called a *cornea* (COR nee a). The cornea acts like a lens, gathering up light and pinpointing it to the center of the eye. Like a lens, it bulges outward toward the center. You can feel this bulge if you close your eye and press your finger lightly on the lid. Rotate your eye from side to side.

The dark spot in the middle of the eye is called the pupil. Light passes through this spot to the interior space. You have noticed that the pupil spends some of the time the size of a pencil point, and some of the time more like the size of the eraser at the other end.

How does it do it?

Like any well-equipped window, it has a curtain that can adjust for bright and dim light. The eye's curtain is called the *iris* (EYE ris). This ring of colored material, with the help of a whole set of tiny muscles, opens up and shuts down in response to light conditions — automatically.

Just inside the iris is a clear disc called the lens. In fact, it is so clear that you don't notice it covering the pupil. This lens looks like a lens on a magnifying glass, only smaller. Together with the cornea, the lens gathers up light and focuses it to a special light-sensitive spot at the back of the eye.

This light-sensitive spot is called the *retina* (RHET tin ah). It is coated with special cells called rods and cones, which convert light into nerve impulses. These are sent along to the brain by the optic nerve.

90

Eye Observation Step right up and have a good look at your own eyes. Here are some get-acquainted exercises that will make you familiar with various parts of your windows on the world.

CORNEA - THE CORNEA STICKS OUT AWAY FROM THE EYE A SURPRISING DISTANCE.

PUT YOUR FINGER OVER A CLOSED EYE LID. TURN YOUR EYE FROM CORNER TO CORNER. THE LUMP YOU FEEL IS THE CORNEA.

LENS - THE LENS IN THE EYE CAN FOCUS BY BECOMING FATTER OR THINNER. YOU CAN FEEL THE ADJUSTMENTS.

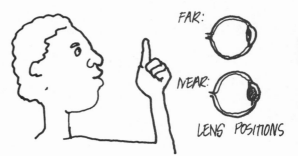

FAR:

NEAR:

LENS POSITIONS

FOCUS A FINGER ABOUT 6" FROM YOUR EYES. BRING IT SLOWLY CLOSER, KEEPING THE RIDGES IN FOCUS. CAN YOU FEEL THE STRAIN?

IRIS - IN BRIGHT CONDITIONS THE IRIS LETS IN ONLY A TINY AMOUNT OF LIGHT. IN DIM CONDITIONS IT CAN OPEN TO LET IN 40 TIMES MORE. WATCH IT AT WORK.

A MAGNIFYING MIRROR IS HELPFUL

STAY IN A DARK PLACE FOR A FEW MINUTES. SHINE A LIGHT INTO YOUR EYES AND WATCH YOUR IRIS SHUT DOWN.

BLIND SPOT - DID YOU KNOW THAT YOU WERE A LITTLE BLIND? THE SPOT ON THE RETINA WHERE THE OPTIC NERVE CONNECTS HAS NO LIGHT RECEPTORS.

① COVER YOUR LEFT EYE.
② LOOK AT THE CROSS WITH YOUR RIGHT EYE.
③ SLOWLY BRING THE PAGE CLOSER.

Eye Dissection   If you don't mind being stared at while you work, you will find this eye dissection to be fascinating. It may be difficult obtaining a sheep or beef eye, but it's worth the trouble. If you have no luck with your local butcher, try a slaughterhouse or meatpacker.

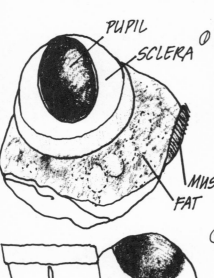

PUPIL

SCLERA

MUSCLE

FAT

① LOOK AT THE EYE. YOU WILL FIND THAT THE EYEBALL SITS IN A MASS OF MUSCLE AND FAT WHICH MOVE AND CUSHION THE EYE. TURN IT OVER AND YOU WILL SEE THE OPTIC NERVE.

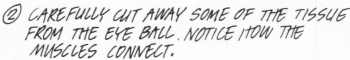

② CAREFULLY CUT AWAY SOME OF THE TISSUE FROM THE EYE BALL. NOTICE HOW THE MUSCLES CONNECT.

③ SLICE ACROSS THE TOUGH CORNEA. A THIN LIQUID CALLED THE AQUEOUS HUMOR WILL SEEP OUT. THE LENS SITS UNDER THE IRIS. RE-MOVE IT.

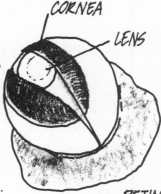

CORNEA

LENS

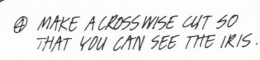

④ MAKE A CROSSWISE CUT SO THAT YOU CAN SEE THE IRIS.

⑤ ENLARGE THE CUTS SO YOU CAN SEE THE RETINA AT THE BACK OF THE EYE. SCOOP OUT THE CLEAR JELLY (VITREOUS HUMOR). FIND THE BLIND SPOT WHERE THE OPTIC NERVE CONNECTS.

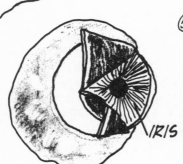

IRIS

RETINA

CAPILLARIES

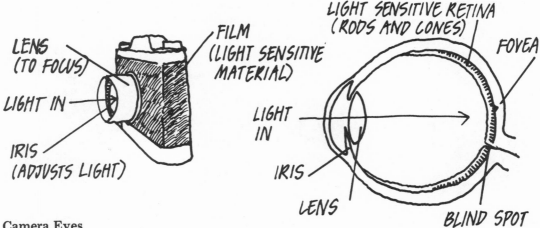

LENS (TO FOCUS)

LIGHT IN

IRIS (ADJUSTS LIGHT)

FILM (LIGHT SENSITIVE MATERIAL)

LIGHT SENSITIVE RETINA (RODS AND CONES)

FOVEA

LIGHT IN

IRIS

LENS

BLIND SPOT

Camera Eyes

In many ways the eye is like a camera. Light streams into a dark chamber through a lens onto a film of light-sensitive material.

Unlike a camera, the light-sensitive material in the eye takes two different kinds of pictures at the same time. In a way, you see twice with one eye.

The light-sensitive retina has two kinds of light receivers. They are named after their shapes. One group is called rods. The other is called cones.

Rods are in charge of black and white or light and dark vision. They are very sensitive to light.

Cones take care of color vision. They are sensitive to different colors of light. However, they need much more light than the rods do to activate them.

Rods and cones are not scattered around helter-skelter inside the eye like nuts and chocolate chips inside a cookie. They are organized in a special way that has a great deal to do with how you see the world.

Photo Cells

The retina covers an area about the size of a postage stamp inside the back of the eye.

The rods are scattered over all parts of the retina but are concentrated toward the outer edges.

The cones are mostly toward the center of the retina and reach a very high concentration in a little pit called the *fovea* (FO vee ah).

The fovea is directly in line with the lens, so a focused light image of the outside world touches the retina exactly here. The many receptors allow a very fine image to be picked up and sent to the brain. The photo sensors in the fovea are responsibile for your sharp, focused vision.

Information from both rods and cones is sent to the brain where it is read as one picture. However, sometimes the rod vision is more important, and sometimes the cone vision is more important.

Shifty-Eyed   You probably think you see the world very clearly. In fact, you can only focus on one tiny spot at any one time. This exercise will make you aware of why we are all shifty eyed.

① OPEN THIS BOOK AT RANDOM. FOCUS YOUR EYES ON ANY WORD. <u>WITHOUT</u> MOVING YOUR EYES TRY AND READ THE SURROUNDING WORDS.

② NOW FOCUS ON SOMETHING ACROSS THE ROOM. <u>WITHOUT</u> MOVING YOUR EYES TRY AND SEE THE DETAILS AROUND YOUR FOCUS POINT.

• JUST HOW MUCH DO YOU SEE AT A GLANCE?
• WHAT'S THIS GOT TO DO WITH YOUR FOVEA?

Sight at Night   Rods do a rather poor job of defining details. But they earn first-class honors working in low-light situations. Rod vision is what keeps you from going bump in the night. It is easy to get into the habit of only trusting your clear, focused vision. Here is an experiment that will change your mind.

OBSERVE THE SKY FROM A DARK PLACE.

① AT NIGHT SITE A STAR THAT IS BARELY VISIBLE. LOOK AT IT DIRECTLY.

② NOW LOOK AT IT OUT OF THE CORNER OF YOUR EYE. SEE ANYTHING MORE?

And in This Corner . . .   Your side vision is also called *peripheral* (per RIFF er al) vision. It's the blurry shapes you see from "the corner of your eye." You can easily test how clearly you see with your peripheral vision.

① TEST YOUR PERIPHERAL VISION: OPEN YOUR ARMS BEHIND YOU. MOVE THEM SLOWLY FORWARD. STOP WHEN YOUR FINGERS COME INTO VIEW. DROP SOME CLAY BALLS AS MARKERS. CHART YOUR WIDE ANGLE VISION. IS THERE ANY DIFFERENCE WITH WIGGLING FINGERS?

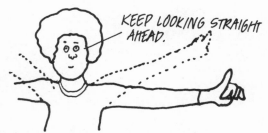

KEEP LOOKING STRAIGHT AHEAD.

USE PAPER SQUARES OF RED, YELLOW, BLUE, BLACK, WHITE, GREEN.
— CLOTHES PIN HOLDER

DRAW AN ARC ON A SHEET OF PAPER. COLOR IN YOUR TEST RESULTS.

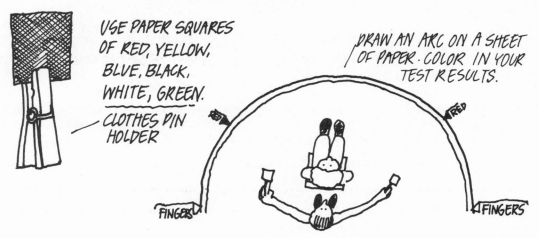

② TEST YOUR PERIPHERAL COLOR VISION. HAVE A FRIEND HOLD UP PAIRS OF COLORED SQUARES. MARK THE RESULTS ON AN ARC CHART LIKE THE ONE ABOVE. SURPRISED?

Eye Color

The coloring of the iris plays an important part in its job as a light screen.

A brown or black iris provides a more effective screen. Peoples of sunnier countries along the equator generally have the dark eyes.

Light eyes, such as blue or green, are an adaptation to the lands of less light.

All babies are born with blue eyes. According to their parentage, their eyes will turn to their permanent color by the time they reach a year old.

Eye Defenses

Before you were born, your eyes were formed out of a bit of brain tissue that migrated to the front of your head. Sitting up there in the middle of your face, these delicate tissues are dangerously exposed.

Eyes have several kinds of protective devices.

First, very little of the eyeball is exposed. It nestles in a bony hollow in the skull called the socket. You can feel the edges of these sockets with your fingers.

The eye is shielded by bushy hedgelike growths, the brows and lashes.

The eyelid clamps down, covering the eye at the slightest hint of an intrusion. Its flapping up and down helps wash the surface with a salty, germ-killing fluid called tears.

Special Events

See Stars. The light-sensitive cells that make up the retina can be excited by pressure. You can cause pressure flashes by gently pressing your eyes. Sometimes a good crack on the head will cause this effect of seeing stars and patterns. (Actually, they look more like flying dots of light rather than pointy stars.)

Amazing Facts

— On the inside corner of the eye, humans have a remnant of an extra eyelid. In some animals this lid closes from the center outward, giving extra protection.

— Animals without stereo vision have no need to see the same picture with both eyes. Their eyes move independently.

— Under good conditions the human eye can distinguish 10 million color surfaces.

Ears

RECEIVERS FOR VIBES FROM THE OUTSIDE

Sound is vibration moving through a material like air, water, or earth. Sometimes you can feel these vibrations. You know this if you have ever stood next to a monster machine that made the ground rumble with its mighty engine noises. You also noticed that the machine was filling the air with vibrations. When vibrations reach your ears, you hear them as sound.

How the Ear Hears

The thing that most people call an ear is only the outskirts. Most of your ear, certainly all the really important parts, are on the inside. The fleshy, cup-shaped flaps on either side of your head and the passages into them are called the outer ear. Their job is to gather up sounds and to direct them down the ear canals.

Some animals, like jackasses and rabbits, have great, large, magnificent ears. What's more, they are adjustable so the animal can get the best possible reception of incoming sounds.

Humans, on the other hand, have rather shrunken, flat, and altogether insignificant-looking ears, which only in the rarest cases can be wiggled even a millimeter. Some scientists say our ears have been scaled down to play seconds to our most developed sense — vision.

After a sound has been caught by the *auricle* (ORE ick cull) — the official name for the ear flap — it begins its way down the ear canal. The openings to these tunnels look like dark caves on either side of your head.

At the end of the canal is the eardrum, a tissue very much like a skin stretched over a drum. A sound passing down the ear canal causes the drum to vibrate.

The vibrations are passed on by the drum to three tiny bones. The first, called the hammer, is attached to the drum. It passes vibes on to the anvil, which sends them to the stirrup. The purpose of this mini-relay system is to magnify the gentle sounds and soften the loud sounds.

97

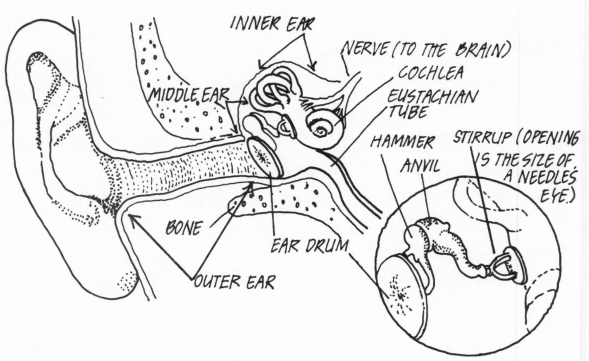

Vibrations from the stirrup are passed on to the *cochlea* (COKE lee a), a snail-shaped passage carved in the bone and filled with fluid. Vibrations in this fluid are picked up by hairlike things which extend into the fluid. They respond to these vibrations by sending nerve signals to the brain, where they are perceived as sound.

Silent Dog Whistle?

Dogs have the ability to hear higher-pitched sounds than humans. In fact, much of bird songs and bat noises are silence to our ears because they fall into ranges beyond our hearing. Check the chart to see where various sounds fall in relation to each other.

HUMANS CAN HEAR SOUNDS BETWEEN 20 AND ABOUT 16,000 CYCLES PER SECOND. (THE DARK AREA ON THIS CHART.)

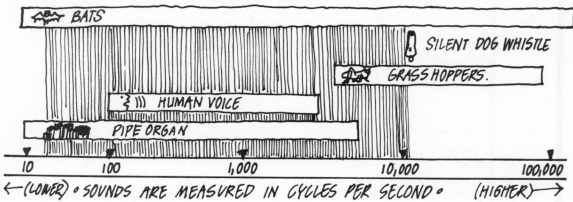

Soundscope   You can actually see the sound of your own voice with this easy-to-make instrument. The membrane responds to sound much like your own eardrum. You can learn something about sound vibration, voice, and eardrums, plus have a good time, with this simple tin can device.

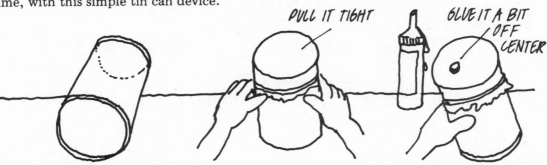

PULL IT TIGHT

GLUE IT A BIT OFF CENTER

① CUT THE TOP AND THE BOTTOM FROM A SOUP CAN.

② STRETCH A PIECE OF BALLOON OVER AN END SECURE IT WITH A RUBBER BAND.

③ GLUE A SMALL PIECE OF BROKEN MIRROR ON THE MEMBRANE.

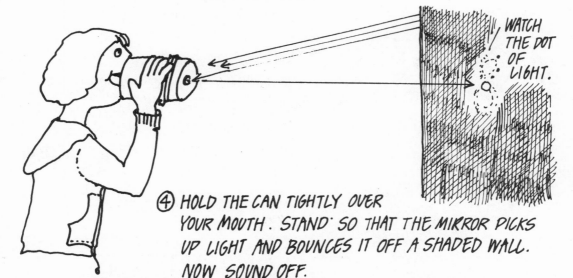

WATCH THE DOT OF LIGHT.

④ HOLD THE CAN TIGHTLY OVER YOUR MOUTH. STAND SO THAT THE MIRROR PICKS UP LIGHT AND BOUNCES IT OFF A SHADED WALL. NOW SOUND OFF.

○ HOW DO THE PATTERNS CHANGE FOR HIGH AND LOW SOUNDS?

○ WHAT DOES "CYCLES PER SECOND" MEAN?

○ FIND OUT WHAT THE DIFFERENCE IS BETWEEN PITCH AND LOUDNESS. (HOW DO THEY LOOK?)

○ HOW IS THE SOUNDSCOPE MEMBRANE LIKE AN EAR DRUM?

Fifteen Minutes on the Ear Canal

Fifteen Minutes on the Ear Canal You can't look down your own ear canals, but you can look at a friend's. If your friend has really straight canals, all you need is a flashlight. Earcups for an otoscope (the ear observation device a doctor uses) will make looking a lot easier. You can buy them from a hospital supply, or perhaps you can ask your doctor for a few.

① USE A PEN FLASHLIGHT OR MAKE A CONE TO TURN A REGULAR FLASHLIGHT INTO ONE WITH A NARROW BEAM.

OTOSCOPE CUPS COME IN SIZES. USE SMALL FOR CHILDREN'S EARS.

CUT A PAPER CIRCLE.

FOLD IT INTO A CONE. TAPE IT ONTO THE LIGHT.

SLIT

RULE ONE: BE GENTLE!

② FIRST HAVE A LOOK WITHOUT THE CUP. PULL THE LOBE UPWARDS TO STRAIGHTEN THE CANAL. IF YOU RUN INTO A LOT OF EARWAX, YOU MIGHT SUGGEST, TACTFULLY OF COURSE, THAT YOUR PARTNER WASH HIS/HER EARS, SO YOU CAN CONTINUE YOUR OBSERVATION.

③ GENTLY PLACE THE CUP IN THE EAR, USING IT TO DIRECT THE LIGHT TOWARD THE INSIDE.

BE PATIENT. FINDING THE EARDRUM ISN'T ALWAYS EASY. IF YOU HAD NO LUCK, TRY SOMEONE WITH STRAIGHTER CANALS.

THE INSIDE OF THE CANAL WILL LOOK PINK AND DAMP. THE DRUM WILL LOOK A SHINEY, PEARL GRAY COLOR.

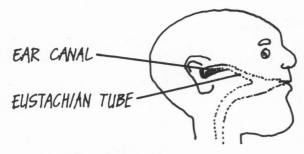

EAR CANAL

EUSTACHIAN TUBE

Eustachian Tubes

The eardrum is a delicate part of your hearing equipment. Like a blown-up balloon, or any stretched material, it runs the risk of tearing if too much stress is put on it.

Like most of your body's machines, your eardrum has a safety system to prevent a disaster. This system consists of the *Eustachian* (u STA shun) tubes. They lead from the space behind your eardrum and are connected to your nose and throat. You and your Eustachian tubes are most likely old friends. They are what gives you that funny, flat feeling behind your ears when you go up in a plane or an elevator, or come down a mountain. When they open suddenly, we say, "My ears popped." However, that's precisely what they guard against.

When you change altitude, the air pressure changes too. (Remember, air is thinner high up.) Air begins to press unequally on the eardrums. If the difference is too great, the drum will break to equalize the pressure. To prevent this, the Eustachian tubes provide an air passage to get air behind your drums that is of the same pressure as the air pressing in from the outside.

A yawn or swallow helps move air in its equalization process. If a tremendous pressure can't be equalized quickly enough, the drum will tear. These small slits are usually not too serious and will heal.

101

Are Two Ears Better Than One?

It is true that in the case of some vital organs we have more than enough. For instance, a person can survive with one lung or lead quite a normal life with only one kidney. But, how would you do with only one ear? Here is an experiment to try so you can find out what the other ear is for.

① PLACE YOURSELF AT A DISTANCE AT WHICH YOUR PARTNER CAN JUST HEAR THE TICKING OF A WATCH.

② BLINDFOLD YOUR PARTNER. TEST THEIR ABILITY TO TELL THE DIRECTION OF THE TICKING. TAKE TEN POSITIONS. KEEP TRACK.

V = RIGHT
X = WRONG

BE VERY QUIET CHANGING POSITIONS.

③ HAVE THE BLINDFOLDED PERSON PLUG ONE EAR. TRY TEN MORE MORE POSITIONS. ANY CONCLUSIONS?

Sound Source

A blind person can tell the direction of a sound for two reasons — their ears.

A sound coming from an unknown direction is heard a split second sooner in one ear than in the other (about 1/1,500 of a second sooner). Also, the head acts as a sound barrier, so a noise is a little louder in one ear than in the other. These tiny differences can be analyzed by the brain — not to mention your years of practice — to locate the sound's direction.

Another interesting effect is echolocation. Large objects tend to reflect sounds. This bounce-back effect is called an echo. Blindfolded you will find that you have a surprising amount of echolocation ability. For instance, walking along, you might detect a wall from the changing sound of your footsteps. Which leads to the question: Why do blind people never wear sneakers?

**Musical Bones
(or, Bones and Overtones)**

If you ever heard a recording of your voice, you probably didn't believe it was your own. Everyone else said yours was exactly true to life, though the recorder really messed up when it taped their own voices.

The trick your own voice plays on you has to do with an effect called "bone resonance." What it means is that you not only hear your voice through your ears, but through your own bones as well. Some sound vibrations travel through your own skull and vibrate the cochlea directly, bypassing your ears in the process. So your own bones give your voice certain overtones that are heard by you alone.

Don't believe it? You can prove it yourself with a fork.

Tuning Fork Test   The best equipment for this experiment is a tuning fork. The next best thing is a big, all-metal kitchen fork; an all-metal table fork will do, except the sound isn't as loud.

① STRIKE THE TINES ON A METAL SURFACE. MAKE THE LOUDEST TONE YOU CAN.

② HOLD IT NEXT TO YOUR EAR UNTIL YOU CAN HARDLY HEAR IT.

③ QUICKLY PLACE THE HANDLE BETWEEN YOUR TEETH.

• WHAT DOES THIS TELL YOU ABOUT HOW SOUND TRAVELS?

◦ SEE IF SOUND CAN TRAVEL ALONG OTHER PATHWAYS.

**The Inside Story on an Old Wives'
Seaside Tale**

You now know that all sound pathways
are not through the ear. Did you ever
think that the blood rushing through the
vessels in your inner ear might set up vibrations that would cause a lot of distract-
ing noise? Luckily, your body has solved
this problem you didn't know you had
by designing your ears in such a way that
most of this noise is reduced.

But under very quiet conditions, you *can*
hear the hum of your own pulse. In fact,
the old trick of putting a shell to your ear
to "listen to the sea" creates those quiet
conditions that magnify the sound of
blood rushing by your inner ear.

Amazing Facts

— The smallest bones in the body are
located in the ear.

— Children have the best hearing. Their
ears are sensitive to the higher sounds.
This high-pitched sensitivity is gradually
lost with age.

— Human ears have a tremendous loudness
range. Factory noise is one million times
as loud as a soft whisper.

— Loud noises, or sounds of many decibels,
can permanently damage the ears. In fact,
sounds over 175 decibels can cause death.

Balance
THE SENSE OF UPRIGHT

Bet you can't keep still for a minute. Try it for yourself with the balance experiment on the next page.

Not easy is it?

Standing still is hard work. Balancing is a full-time operation. Your muscles are constantly struggling to keep you upright.

Stop for a minute and review your situation. Humans are long, tall beings with hardly anything to stand on.

Other land animals have much more sensible support systems. Most go about on four legs, with some exceptions, like the kangaroo. Even so, the kangaroo's tripod footing is more stable than our own. No doubt you have seen a stool with three legs, but have you ever seen one with two?

When you think about it, the decision to walk on two legs was a risky one for our early ancestors. It demands some fancy machinery in the business of balance.

Design Problem

If you were designing a long, tall, two-footed creature, where would you put its balance detectors?

Inner Ear

Your balance sensors are located in your head — inside your ear, next to your cochlea. Actually, your balance sensors are two separate devices that keep track of different sorts of information.

One device is made up of the *utricle* (YOU trick ul) and *saccule* (SAC yool). These are the up-and-down sensors.

105

The other device is made up of the semi-circular canals. These are the change-in-direction sensors.

These sensors have different shapes and functions, but they operate basically the same way. Your balance mechanisms respond to pressure. They are a refined sense of touch.

Up and Down Sense

The utricle and saccule are your organs that sense up and down. Utricle means little bag. Saccule means (you guessed it) little sack. That is exactly what they are — little hair-lined bags containing fluid.

Inside these bags are something called — are you ready? — *otoconia* (oh toe CO nee ah). This means ear dust. This ear dust is actually tiny sand-size crystals of bone material. The otoconia rest on the bottom of the utricle and saccule, sort of like sand at the bottom of a fishbowl.

When you stand on your head, the gravity will pull the ear dust right off the bottom, onto what was the top of your ear spheres. The sensitive hairs detect a change and send a message to the brain.

Besides sensing a shift in up and down, these hair cells can also detect a change in speed. The feeling of moving forward is caused by the otoconia lagging behind. The hair cells bend backward as the body goes forward.

You know from riding in a car that this sensation lasts only a few seconds. Once you've started moving for a few moments, your otoconia catch up. You lose the sensation of motion until you stop, when the reverse happens.

The Will to Keep Still   A sure way to make some gum money is to bet a friend that he can't keep still for two minutes. Follow these instructions to make sure they don't move a millimeter.

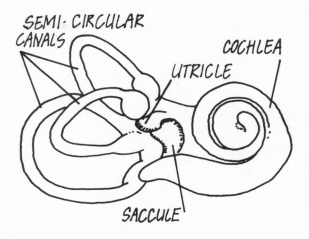

SEMI-CIRCULAR CANALS

COCHLEA

UTRICLE

SACCULE

Each of the canals is located so it occupies three different planes, a handy arrangement, since we live in a three-dimensional world.

When you turn your head, the liquid inside one or more of the canals presses against the hairs. Your brain receives a signal that your head is beginning to turn. As you stop turning, the fluid presses against the hairs a different way. This signals the brain that you are stopping the turn.

Sometimes, after some violent moving, the fluid inside your balance sensors will stay in motion for a few moments after your head has stopped. You know you have stopped, but according to the signals from your inner ear, it still feels like the world is spinning. You have a case of the dizzies. Until your inner ears calm, it would be wise to sit down before you fall down.

Sense of Direction

The semicircular canals detect changes in the direction of movement. These three hair-lined, liquid-filled tubes sit just next to the utricle and saccule. They are named for their shape, which is semicircular.

Lag-Behind Effect You can demonstrate for yourself that fluid does lag behind in a moving vessel. Prove it with a glass of water. You can experience the sensation caused by this effect in your ears. Just jiggle your head.

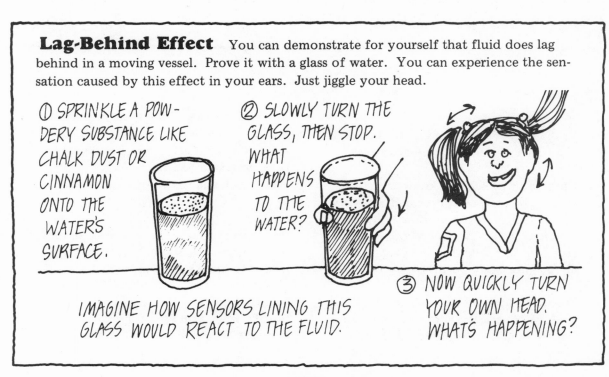

① SPRINKLE A POWDERY SUBSTANCE LIKE CHALK DUST OR CINNAMON ONTO THE WATER'S SURFACE.

② SLOWLY TURN THE GLASS, THEN STOP. WHAT HAPPENS TO THE WATER?

③ NOW QUICKLY TURN YOUR OWN HEAD. WHAT'S HAPPENING?

IMAGINE HOW SENSORS LINING THIS GLASS WOULD REACT TO THE FLUID.

Upright Without Sight

Just how important is your eyesight in keeping your balance? Here are two tests. The first distorts the visual information. The second does away with it altogether. Ready? Steady?

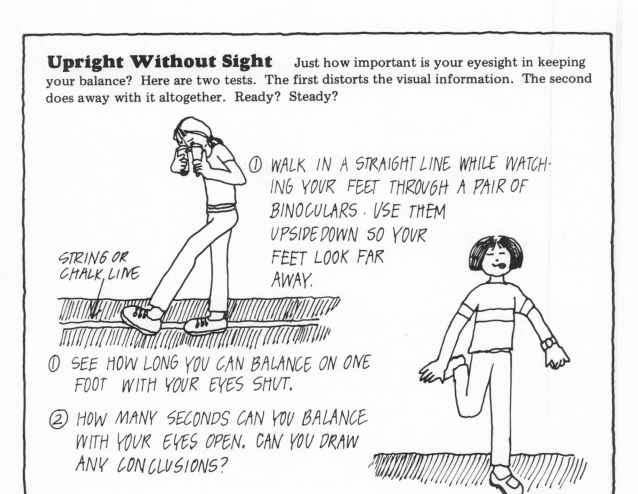

① WALK IN A STRAIGHT LINE WHILE WATCHING YOUR FEET THROUGH A PAIR OF BINOCULARS. USE THEM UPSIDE DOWN SO YOUR FEET LOOK FAR AWAY.

STRING OR CHALK LINE

① SEE HOW LONG YOU CAN BALANCE ON ONE FOOT WITH YOUR EYES SHUT.

② HOW MANY SECONDS CAN YOU BALANCE WITH YOUR EYES OPEN. CAN YOU DRAW ANY CONCLUSIONS?

Quick Shifts

Could you stand up and move around if your balance sensors were destroyed?

Close your eyes. You know without looking where your knees and elbows are. This is called your *kinesthetic* (KIN ess thet ick) sense. It comes from nerve sensors in your joints that tell your brain about your body position.

Also, you have pressure receptors in the soles of your feet. They tell you how your weight is distributed on them.

This information, combined with information from your eyes, is enough to keep you walking a straight and narrow path, *provided you do it slowly*. However, quick changes in balance require a full set of inner ear apparatus.

Information from your balance sensors to the automatic muscular control center in the brain stem can correct for any imbalance *before* it happens. These are balance reflexes. This is a handy talent to have when you are walking on an icy sidewalk or learning to ride a bike.

Whirls Your automatic balance control system tends to set your muscles into action to counter any upsetting movements. Give your balance reflexes a whirl with this experiment:

① SPIN YOURSELF AND A FRIEND. IN WHAT DIRECTION DO YOU LEAN? ANY IDEA WHY?

② A PERSON SPUN QUICKLY ON A SWIVEL CHAIR OR SWING WILL SHOW TO AND FRO MOTIONS OF THE EYES. ALSO THEY WILL FEEL LIKE THEY ARE SPINNING, EVEN AFTER THEY HAVE STOPPED. WHY?

Incredible Balancing Act

When you start to fall, a foot whips out to catch you. When you run, you lean forward to counterbalance the force of air pressing against you as you speed along. When you stop short, your arms fly up and you throw your weight backwards.

Any sort of movement demands counter-motions in the opposite direction. This automatic, lightning-quick play of muscle motion and countermotion is called the balance reflexes.

The only time you give this incredible balancing act any notice is during those rare times when some error has landed you on your nose. First you check the damage, then you look around to see if anyone has noticed how silly you look sprawled on the ground. Instead of picking yourself up and marvelling at what a fantastic job your body does most of the time, you get angry with your stupid feet for falling down on the job.

What Is Balance?

All parts of your body have weight. When you're standing still, all this weight balances, like a pencil on your finger or two people on a seesaw. Of course, you get some help from your feet, which act like an anchor. If you move suddenly, an extra force acts on that part of you that moved, like your leg if you've just kicked a ball. To stay balanced, you have to shift some part of you to counter this extra force.

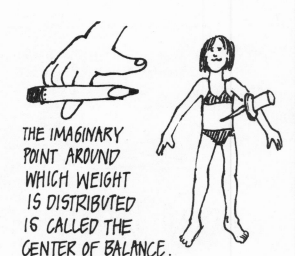

THE IMAGINARY POINT AROUND WHICH WEIGHT IS DISTRIBUTED IS CALLED THE CENTER OF BALANCE.

Equilibrium Appreciation

Your body constantly performs an astounding, everchanging array of feats of balance — and you never give it the slightest thought. When your body keeps its balance, it is described as maintaining *equilibrium* (ee qua LIB ree um). Try these exercises in equilibrium appreciation:

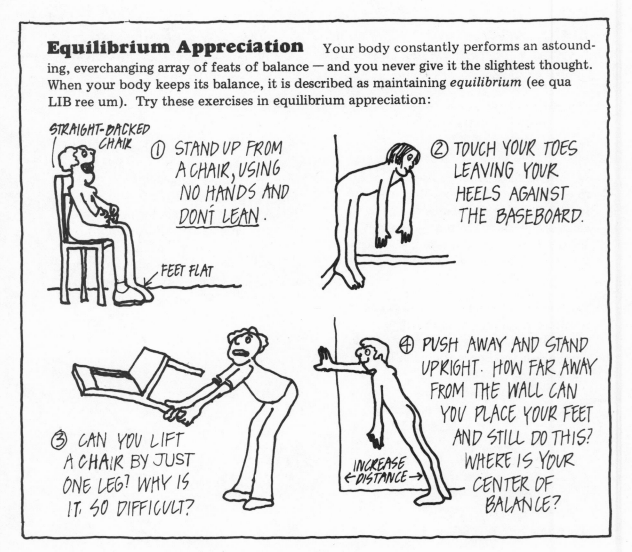

STRAIGHT-BACKED CHAIR

① STAND UP FROM A CHAIR, USING NO HANDS AND DON'T LEAN.

FEET FLAT

② TOUCH YOUR TOES LEAVING YOUR HEELS AGAINST THE BASEBOARD.

③ CAN YOU LIFT A CHAIR BY JUST ONE LEG? WHY IS IT SO DIFFICULT?

④ PUSH AWAY AND STAND UPRIGHT. HOW FAR AWAY FROM THE WALL CAN YOU PLACE YOUR FEET AND STILL DO THIS? WHERE IS YOUR CENTER OF BALANCE?

←INCREASE DISTANCE→

Brain and Nervous System
MISSION CONTROL

Picture yourself walking around a corner counting cracks in the sidewalk. Someone shouts. You look up to find you are about to be run down by a crazy person on a fast skateboard.

Your eyes widen.

Your muscles tighten.

You gasp.

Your heart jumps.

In a split second your brain has sized up your plight. Suddenly your muscles send you flying into a bush, safe. All before you knew what was happening.

Then you see that the lunatic was your brother. "You jerk! I won't forget this!" you yell. Your mind starts planning how to get even.

These lightning reactions were the work of your nervous system, the body's mission control. In less than a second, about one hundred thousand nerve cells relayed all sorts of signals to move you out of harm's way.

When your nervous system isn't responding to emergencies, it coordinates the normal work of your trillions of cells. It keeps tabs on your internal operations, as well as what goes on in the world outside your skin. It senses changes in the environment and makes the necessary adjustments. It keeps things running smoothly and on course, both inside and out.

Getting Ahead

The basic job of a nervous system is to be irritable. Irritability means the ability to sense changes in the environment and to adjust to them. Irritability is a basic survival skill.

Even simple, bloblike animals like jellyfish are irritable. They have nervous systems that are arranged in a netlike way, all over their bodies.

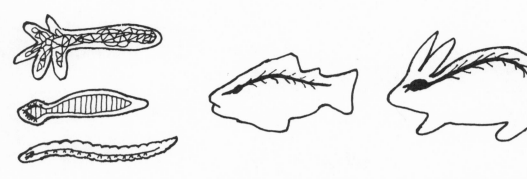

More complex animals have a different sort of body plan, a plan in which one side is built the same as the other. We call this bilateral symmetry. For example, worms are the simplest multi-celled creatures with bilateral symmetry.

Bilaterally symmetric creatures no longer drifted every which way. Their lives had direction. Their nervous systems got bigger and much more sophisticated. An onslaught of new information had to be dealt with by these creatures, like how to move along in a particular direction. Gradually, a knot of nervous tissue developed at the end of the body facing the unknown. This became the first brain.

Later, mammals developed ever bigger brains to deal with ever more complex worlds of sight, smell, and sound; not to mention internal controls like temperature and equilibrium.

Still, the basic plan borrows a lot from our worm cousins. Our brains are nothing more than enormous knots of nerve cells at the end of the nerve highway.

Nerve Highway

All animal nerves work the same way. They are cells with skinny arms that make up a body-wide network. They fire tiny electric charges — which are the body's messengers — along the nerve highway.

This network is made up of nerve cells, or *neurons* (NOOR ons) for short. Each nerve is able to build up a tiny electric charge by mixing chemicals within itself. It fires off the charge across a tiny space to the next nerve cell. This cell then fires off a charge to the next cell along the nerve highway. All this action takes place in a split second. Each nerve cell is quickly ready to recharge and fire again. In fact, a nerve can send up to one thousand impulses per second.

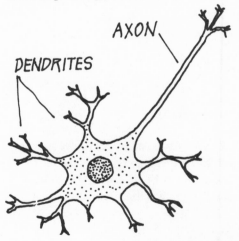

A nerve cell has a special shape. It looks something like a spider hanging from the ceiling. The long arm is called an *axon* (AX on). The shorter ones are called *dendrites* (DEN drytes). Nerve messages always travel through the cell from dendrite to axon.

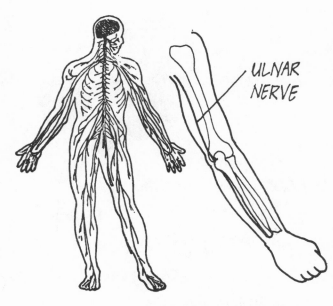

ULNAR NERVE

What we call a nerve is actually a bundle of these many-armed cells, which make up long strings of nerve fibers. These link up all parts of the body. The nerve highway system is made up of 12,000 million nerve cells.

You can think of a nerve highway made up of kids holding hands. Each is one nerve cell. Impulses don't flow smoothly like water out of a hose. They go in spurts. Like passing along a hand squeeze.

Funny Bone

Nerve tissue is soft and easily damaged. Most of it is behind bony protections or deep within muscle tissue. One exception is the ulnar nerve, which occupies the little hollow at your elbow. Sometimes if you hit it just right . . .

Ever knock your elbow and get that electric needles-and-pins feeling, as if you have been shocked? Well, in a way you have.

Bone Dome

Our human brains are the latest model in millions of years of testing and researching by evolution. Some parts of our brain, like the core and spinal cord, are similar to the entire brains of simpler creatures like fishes or reptiles. Sometimes these are called the "old" brain parts because they developed early in the history of animals. Other parts of our human brain are only found in more advanced mammals. This is the equipment that allows us to survive in a more complex world. We call these the "new" brain parts.

The new parts developed on top of the older, more primitive brain, expanding the brain upward. People like to call the jobs of the newer parts the "higher" functions.

Have a look around the animal kingdom and take notice of that important space above the eyebrows.

Up the Control Tower

Ask somebody to describe the brain, and they will tell you all about the big, wrinkled, walnut-looking thing. They never mention the older parts hidden under its folds, the stem, or the spinal cord.

Strictly speaking, all of this is brain tissue. Each part performs a special job in your control system. While no one is sure exactly how the brain works, we do know that the older and less-conscious jobs happen in the lower, less-evolved brain parts.

Actions like dropping a hot potato are controlled in the spinal cord. These quick responses are called reflexes. They are finished before you know what happened.

The base of the brain handles many of those actions that you never notice. Things like keeping your feet from getting tangled up when you walk, keeping your intestines churning, or making your mouth water.

Deep within the brain is the ancient forebrain. This is the part of the brain that wants to punch the punk kid that stepped on your lunch. Here is the seat of conscious emotions like fear, anger, and the urge to mate. It is also involved with sensations like hunger, thirst, and smell.

The top of your brain, or *cerebrum* (sa REE brum), is the big wrinkly part. This is the part that decided it wasn't such a good idea to punch that kid, because she was bigger and tougher than you. This is the site of your memory, imagination, reasoning ability, and voluntary control. It is the most human part of your brain.

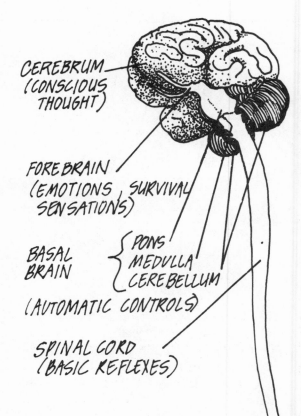

CEREBRUM
(CONSCIOUS THOUGHT)

FOREBRAIN
(EMOTIONS, SURVIVAL SENSATIONS)

BASAL BRAIN

{ PONS
MEDULLA
CEREBELLUM

(AUTOMATIC CONTROLS)

SPINAL CORD
(BASIC REFLEXES)

Brain Watching
(or, Thinking About Thinking)

Have you ever watched a sad movie and not wanted to cry because you felt silly? Then your emotional parts went ahead and cried anyway, even though your cerebral parts kept telling you it was only a stupid movie.

Did you ever want to stay mad at somebody, but couldn't? Or get too mad to think straight? Or too scared to move? Or so excited you couldn't sleep?

Have you ever wanted a fourth piece of birthday cake, even though your sensible self told you you were crazy?

Listen in on what's happening inside your brain. Watch yourself. You might be surprised at what you find out.

Brain Dissection

Unlike looking at a heart or an eye, examining the brain won't give many clues to how it operates. Still, you might find it interesting to take a closeup look at the most complex and mysterious of organs. Beef brains come to the butcher in big bags. By the time they arrive they are somewhat scrambled, so you might have to settle for two halves and assorted parts. Better, order one from a meat packer. Ask for one with the stem attached.

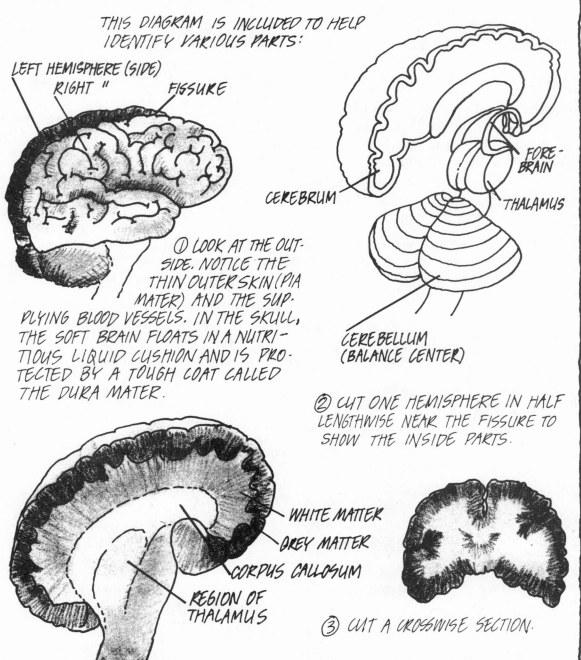

THIS DIAGRAM IS INCLUDED TO HELP IDENTIFY VARIOUS PARTS:

LEFT HEMISPHERE (SIDE)
RIGHT "
FISSURE

FORE-BRAIN
THALAMUS
CEREBRUM
CEREBELLUM (BALANCE CENTER)

① LOOK AT THE OUTSIDE. NOTICE THE THIN OUTER SKIN (PIA MATER) AND THE SUPPLYING BLOOD VESSELS. IN THE SKULL, THE SOFT BRAIN FLOATS IN A NUTRITIOUS LIQUID CUSHION AND IS PROTECTED BY A TOUGH COAT CALLED THE DURA MATER.

② CUT ONE HEMISPHERE IN HALF LENGTHWISE NEAR THE FISSURE TO SHOW THE INSIDE PARTS.

WHITE MATTER
GREY MATTER
CORPUS CALLOSUM
REGION OF THALAMUS

③ CUT A CROSSWISE SECTION.

Reflexes

Flash a hand in front of your eyes. You blink.

Poke someone with a pin, they jerk away.

Stroke the soles of a baby's foot, and its toes turn down.

All of these reactions are called reflexes. A reflex is an automatic reaction to some sense message, like pain. The information gets processed in your spinal cord. Your muscles react before your brain gets the news of what's happening. This bypass is called a reflex arc.

OOH, THAT WAS HOT.

A NERVE MESSAGE WAS RECEIVED BY THE ARM BEFORE THE BRAIN KNEW WHAT HAPPENED.

Knee Jerker The nerve signals for a knee jerk can travel over two pathways. One starts in the brain and travels along the spine, down through the leg. This is a conscious, or voluntary command. The other is a reflex arc started by the tap test.

SIDE OF HAND JUST BELOW THE KNEE

KICK!

① YOU CAN START A REFLEX ACTION BY TAPPING JUST BELOW THE KNEE. YOU MAY HAVE TO TRY SEVERAL SPOTS BEFORE YOU ARE ON TARGET.

② GIVE BOTH A SOUND SIGNAL AND A TAP SIGNAL FOR THE KNEE JERK.
o WHICH ONE SEEMS TO TAKE LONGER?
o WHY?

Limb Levitation

Kids have been teaching each other this trick for a long time. It's sure to amaze your friends who don't know it. All you need for this disarming experiment is a doorway and your own two arms.

① STAND IN A DOORWAY AND PRESS UPWARD <u>AS HARD AS YOU CAN</u> FOR 30 SECONDS.

② RELAX YOUR ARMS. THEY HAVE REMAINED PROGRAMED TO RISE, EVEN AFTER YOUR SIGNALS HAVE STOPPED.

Dollar Drop

When you catch a ball, your brain estimates where the ball is going to be in an instant; it then throws up your hands to meet it at that point. To perform a movement, your nervous system needs time to size up a situation and react. Here is a different game of catch:

USE A DOLLAR BILL OR A PIECE OF PAPER CUT TO BILL SIZE.

① DROP THE DOLLAR BILL FROM A HEIGHT ON ITS SIDE, SO IT FLUTTERS AS IT FALLS.

② TRY AND CATCH IT. GIVE YOURSELF FIVE TRIES. (IF THIS IS TOO EASY, USE ONE HAND ONLY.)

• A FALLING DOLLAR BILL MOVES A LOT SLOWER THAN A FOOTBALL PASS. WHY IS IT HARDER TO CATCH?

Smarts

A lot of people seem to think that intelligence is a score you get from taking tests at school. However, tests only cover little bits of your vast and complex nervous system.

Some people are quick learners. Others have great memories. Some are real good at getting answers to math problems — so long as they're not geometry.

Some people are socially smart. They can wrap anybody around their little finger, while other people are always stepping on somebody's toes.

Some people have perfect pitch. There are the mechanical geniuses who can fix anything with a screwdriver and some bubble gum.

Some people write wonderfully creative stories, and still flunk English because they have bad memories when it comes to remembering spelling and commas.

Some people have extraordinary coordination and can perform fantastic gymnastic feats. There are some who have a hard time learning to type.

Some people have great intuition, or a foolproof sense of direction, or unbreakable concentration.

The next time they pass out tests at school, ignore that sinking feeling in your stomach. Remember, you are getting tested on certain abilities — but there are a whole lot of ways to be smart.

INTELLIGENCE IS A HARD THING TO DEFINE. ONE DEFINITION IS THE ABILITY TO THINK ABSTRACTLY. THIS HAPPENS WHEN YOU SIZE UP A NEW SITUATION OR PROBLEM · YOU SHUFFLE THE PARTS AROUND IN YOUR MIND TO COME UP WITH A NEW SOLUTION OR GRASP OF THE SITUATION. HERE IS AN EXAMPLE OF CHIMPANZEE INTELLIGENCE.

Muscle Learning Learning is not all math problems and spelling quizzes. Learning includes things like juggling, typing, walking on your hands, and playing the piano. Like they say, practice makes perfect. This experiment will help you decide if there is muscle learning.

HAND MUST BE FLAT.

① DROP A STONE FROM 10 INCHES. CAN YOUR PARTNER AVOID BEING HIT? IF IT'S TOO EASY, TRY IT FROM 8".

② DROP IT A NUMBER OF TIMES, THEN SWITCH SIDES. DID YOU IMPROVE? DO YOU THINK THAT THERE IS MUSCLE LEARNING?

Force of Habit Habits are formed by doing something again and again until the action is done without conscious effort. The action becomes automatic. Habits can save a lot of thinking time. Prove it for yourself.

① NUMBER A SHEET OF PAPER FROM 1-50. TIME HOW LONG IT TAKES TO WRITE YOUR NAME 50 TIMES.

② TIME YOURSELF AGAIN, ONLY THIS TIME WRITE YOUR NAME BACKWARDS 50 TIMES.

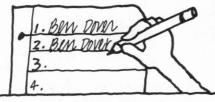

Training Time Habits have a way of happening even when you don't want them to. It takes a lot of effort to unlearn a habit. Here is an exercise in habit breaking.

READ SOMEONE THESE SENTENCES. TELL THEM TO WRITE THEM DOWN QUICKLY, <u>WITHOUT</u> DOTTING THE I'S OR CROSSING THE T'S. TRY IT YOURSELF. IT'S NOT EASY, IS IT?

○ THE RAIN IN SPAIN FALLS MAINLY ON THE PLAIN.

○ TOM ATE FRIED FISH THREE TIMES A WEEK.

○ THERE IS NIT-PICKING TINA.

○ SIMPLE SIMON MET A PIE MAN.

○ TIDDLY WINKS IS A TINY BIT SILLY.

Remember?

Have you ever wondered what it would be like if you woke up each day with a blank memory bank? You would have to search your house to find the bathroom. Every morning you would have to meet your mom and dad all over again. Of course, you could read your favorite stories over and over — if you could remember how to read.

Memory is important. It allows you to form habits so you can think about something else while you tie your shoes. It lets you retain muscle skills. If you fell off a boat today, you wouldn't drown, because you learned how to swim last summer. Once you solve a problem, it's a lot faster next time. Remembering the answer can help you when you come up against a different but similar problem.

No one is certain how the brain remembers. It is thought that information is stored in the cerebral cortex by changes in the brain chemicals.

There seem to be three kinds of memories.

Short-term memories last only seconds. These are fleeting sense impressions, like glancing up and noticing clouds in the sky.

Medium memory is remembering a phone number long enough to dial, or cramming for an exam. These memories may last moments or a few hours.

Long-term memories are the kind that are sorted, sifted, and fixed in your mind. These might include the multiplication tables, a picture of what your mom looks like, or your most embarrassing moment.

Forgetting

Forgetting is not necessarily such a bad thing. Who needs a mind full of old phone numbers? Or the names of all the kids in your kindergarten class? And then there are those embarrassing moments you would rather forget (but probably never will).

Some people say they have bad memories. However, some scientific studies have shown that people forget at a predictable rate. Successful remembering depends upon how well a person learned something in the first place.

This seems to say that bad memories are likely to be cases of inattention. After all, how many times have you forgotten to watch your favorite TV show?

Dominance

If you're given a choice, one particular hand reaches out to dial a telephone or hold a pencil. You are either right- or left-handed. You may have never noticed it, but you also have a dominant foot, eye, side of the face, and even side of the tongue.

Babies tend to reach out for things with one hand. This favored fist is called the precision grip. It means that one of your hands and sides specializes in doing tasks that need special coordination — you may look the same on both sides, but one half of you is a lot more coordinated than the other half.

Taking Sides

Ever try writing your name with your left hand (if you're right-handed)? You know that you can't move the left side of your body with the same ease as the right side. This tendency towards unsymmetrical body coordination is reflected in the brain. The two halves of the brain have, in fact, become specialized.

By the time you are ten years old, one brain side has become dominant. For nine-tenths of the population, the left side of the brain is the dominant side. These people are right-handed. The lefties are dominated by the right side of the brain. This reversal is due to a switching of nerve signals, which occurs in the *corpus callosum* (KOR pus, cal LO sum), the bridge between the two sides.

This bridge is all-important in keeping your right side informed about what your left side is doing. Experiments have shown that if you remove one side of the brain, the other side learns to take over. If you cut the bridge between the two, both sides tend to act separately. Monkeys treated this way can't remember what the other side has learned. Dominance is not only helpful, but it seems to be necessary in keeping both sides of the body running smoothly.

Dominance Tests
Most people are either right- or left-sided. Some people have mixed dominance. Here are some tests to check your dominance patterns.

THUMBS —
QUICKLY FOLD YOUR HANDS. WHICH THUMB IS ON TOP?

FOOT —
HAVE SOMEONE ROLL YOU A KICK BALL. CONCENTRATE ON KICKING IT HARD. WHICH FOOT DID YOU USE?

EYE — ① WITH YOUR RIGHT EYE SHUT, SIGHT ALONG YOUR THUMB TO A DISTANT OBJECT.

LEFT EYE OPEN

② OPEN YOUR RIGHT EYE. IF YOUR THUMB SEEMS TO JUMP RIGHT, YOUR RIGHT EYE IS DOMINANT. IF NOT YOUR LEFT EYE DOMINATES.

YOU ALSO HAVE A DOMINANT EAR, SIDE OF THE FACE, TONGUE, AND LEG. CAN YOU THINK OF WAYS TO TEST THESE?

Mind — Body

The brain is a knot of crinkled nerve tissue floating inside the skull. It can be poked, prodded, weighed, measured, tested, dissected, and inspected. Every human being has more or less the same brain.

Your mind is something else. It wakes, sleeps, imagines, remembers, reasons, and dreams. These are things that can only be weighed and measured after a fashion. The mind still remains one of life's major mysteries. It lives in a flesh and blood thing, the brain. But the mind is clearly something way beyond the stuff from which it is made.

Your mind is your own. You have your own memory bank built from your own personal experiences and associations. You have a language and a culture. A way of receiving and sorting out the world. It's the way you think. The way you decide. It's your talents, your weaknesses. It's what you know and don't know. Your one-of-a-kind mind makes you a one-of-a-kind person. So you're blood and guts — and a whole lot more.

Amazing Facts

— The brain, many times more complex than the best computer, operates on the amount of electric power that would light a 10-watt bulb.

— If the brain was lifted out of the skull and spread out, it would cover a page of a newspaper about two feet square.

— Brains are more watery than blood. About 85% water.

— The brain is an oxygen eater. It weighs about three pounds, or 1/50 of your total adult weight. It uses 25% of the oxygen you take in.

Reproduction

LIFE GOES ON

Every body eventually grows old, wears out, and dies. If life is to go on, it must do so in new bodies. It is necessary for creatures to make more of their own kind, or reproduce, to survive as a species.

There are two basic sorts of reproduction. One is called *asexual* (a SEX you al). This is the sort that happens when a piece of an adult breaks away and develops into a fully grown creature just like the parent. Yeasts, crabgrass, and flatworms all have the ability to break up or bud to form their young.

The other sort is called sexual reproduction. Here two creatures of the same species or kind both contribute to the beginnings of a new life, which grows and eventually develops into a new creature. This offspring has some characteristics of both parents, but is exactly like neither. It is a brand-new, one-of-a-kind member of its species.

Part of the art of staying alive is being able to adapt easily to change. The chances of having the right equipment to cope with changes becomes greatly increased when characteristics of two creatures are inherited by their offspring. Sexual reproduction has been so successful in enabling creatures to adapt to a changing environment that most living things reproduce by this means.

Among animals and plants there are many ways to go about sexual reproduction. Ways as different as flowers and flying fish. However, the basics are the same.

Two partners of a kind are necessary. One is called male, the other is called female.

Males contribute sperm cells. Females contribute egg cells.

Sperms and eggs each contain half the recipe (or genes) to produce a new individual.

A sperm and an egg unite, and . . .

Zygote!

(A zygote is a cell that has the ability to develop into an adult individual, given the right environment. Sometimes it's called a fertilized egg.)

The environments in which offspring develop are different for every species. Plants produce seeds, which need the right combination of sun, soil, and water. Birds lay eggs, which need careful protection and incubation. Mammals — that's humans too — produce egg cells which are incubated inside the female body (so they don't need a hard, protecting shell).

In humans, the fertilized egg grows in the mother's *uterus* (YOU ter us) for nine months. On its birthday, the small infant human gets pushed out of the mother's body through her birth canal, and begins a life separate from its mother.

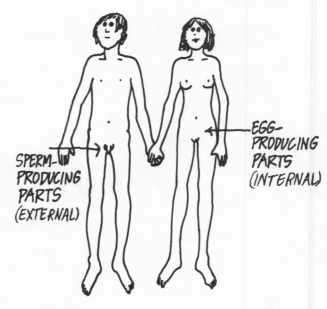

SPERM-PRODUCING PARTS (EXTERNAL)

EGG-PRODUCING PARTS (INTERNAL)

Male-Female

Male and female bodies are basically the same. Bones, organs, breath, life, and death all follow the same patterns. The differences between males and females are directly related to their different jobs in the reproduction business. In reproduction it's the differences that count.

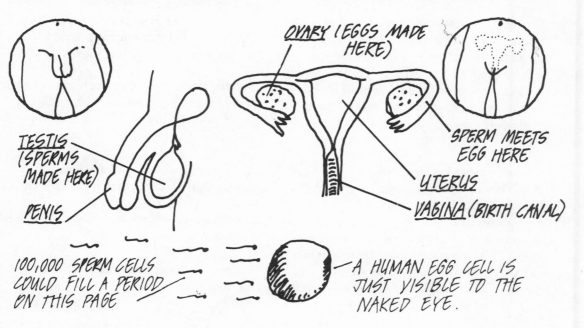

OVARY (EGGS MADE HERE)

TESTIS (SPERMS MADE HERE)

PENIS

SPERM MEETS EGG HERE

UTERUS

VAGINA (BIRTH CANAL)

100,000 SPERM CELLS COULD FILL A PERIOD ON THIS PAGE

A HUMAN EGG CELL IS JUST VISIBLE TO THE NAKED EYE.

Taking Stock Humans are complicated creatures. It is estimated that more than 40,000 genes are needed to produce the intricate recipe that resulted in you. There are many variations that happen within the basic human plan. Some of these variations or traits show up more often than others. Some variations are internal, like blood type. Others are as plain as the nose on your face, or the color of your eyes. Take stock of your own outside variations.

SOME TRAITS ARE DOMINANT. (D)
OTHERS ARE RECESSIVE (R)
THIS MEANS THAT IF YOU INHERIT A GENE FOR BLOND HAIR FROM ONE PARENT, AND A GENE FOR DARK HAIR FROM THE OTHER, CHANCES ARE YOU WILL HAVE DARK HAIR. DARK HAIR IS DOMINANT.

CLOCKWISE HAIR WHORL

D   R

DARK HAIR

D   R

RED HAIR

D   R

WIDOW'S PEAK

D   R

LONG EYE LASHES (3/8" OR MORE)

D   R

DIMPLES

D   R

TURNED-UP NOSE

D   R

Taking Stock (continued)

FREE EAR LOBES

Ⓓ   Ⓡ

EAR POINTS

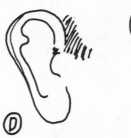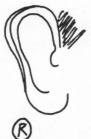

Ⓓ   Ⓡ

HAIR ON MIDDLE JOINTS OF FINGERS

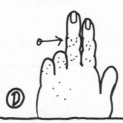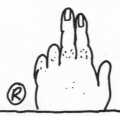

Ⓓ   Ⓡ

FRECKLES

Ⓓ   Ⓡ

BENT LITTLE FINGERS

PRESS

Ⓓ   Ⓡ

EYE COLOR

   Ⓓ DARK    Ⓡ BLUE, GRAY

 Ⓓ HAZEL, GREEN   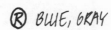 Ⓡ BLUE, GRAY

TONGUE ROLLING - THE ABILITY TO HOLD YOUR TONGUE IN A U SHAPE.

Ⓓ   Ⓡ

TONGUE FOLDING - THE ABILITY TO BEND THE TIP BACK SHARPLY WITHOUT TOUCHING THE TEETH.

Ⓓ   Ⓡ

Chances Are

Have you ever wondered why in creation you are the short one, while the rest of your family are towering giants? Or why you have awful, curly hair, or yukky freckles? Or why you have gorgeous green eyes, while your sister's are dumb old brown?

It all has to do with your genes. Those bits of chemical information you inherited from your parents.

The odds of your parents producing your double are incredibly slim (unless you're an identical twin). These odds are one chance out of a number that is so big it would take you two hours just to write it down (not counting time out for writer's cramp). This number is 1 with 9,031 zeros after it.

Rest assured you're a one-of-a-kind human — a one-time-only combination of freckled, green-eyed, curly-haired shortness.

Which answers one question, but leaves a bigger one —

Why in creation . . . ?